MW01615715

Our
Search
for
Happiness

Our Search for Happiness

AN INVITATION

TO UNDERSTAND

THE CHURCH

OF JESUS CHRIST

OF LATTER-DAY

SAINTS

M. Russell Ballard

M. Russell Ballard

Deseret Book Company
Salt Lake City, Utah

© 1993 M. Russell Ballard

All rights reserved. No part of this book may be reproduced in any form or by any means without permission in writing from the publisher, Deseret Book Company, P. O. Box 30178, Salt Lake City, Utah 84130. This work is not an official publication of The Church of Jesus Christ of Latter-day Saints. The views expressed herein are the responsibility of the author and do not necessarily represent the position of the Church or of Deseret Book Company.

DESERET BOOK is a registered trademark of Deseret Book Company.

Visit us at deseretbook.com

First printing in hardbound, October 1993

First printing in paperbound (Spanish), September 1994

First printing in Missionary Reference Library mass-market edition, December 1994

First printing in paperbound (English), January 1995

ISBN 0-87579-899-3

Printed in the United States of America   8006-0256R
Banta, Menasha, WI

20   19   18   17   16   15   14

To my wife, Barbara,
our children,
and their families

Contents

Acknowledgments

This book has been a long time in the making, and I am indebted to a number of people who have encouraged me and who have contributed to this project in some way. Many colleagues and friends read the manuscript at various stages and made suggestions that strengthened the material significantly. This book is much better because of their contributions.

I am particularly grateful to a number of men and women representing other faiths who willingly read this manuscript. Their reactions and feedback were invaluable in helping me make sure that the message of this book is clear, understandable, and, I hope, not offensive.

While it's always dangerous to single out individual efforts, I greatly appreciate my secretary, Dorothy Anderson, who was tireless in pulling together materials and doing research. Joe Walker's assistance and consultation helped me push the project along. Ron Millett, Eleanor Knowles, Sheri Dew, Kent Ware, and Patricia Parkinson at Deseret Book encouraged this project from the beginning and helped turn a manuscript into a finished volume. And I am likewise grateful to my wife, Barbara, for her patience and loving encouragement.

Despite the contributions and suggestions of many, I alone am fully responsible for the content of this book.

Beginning to Understand

Consider for a moment the word *understanding.*

It's a simple word, really—one that most of us use every day. But it means something that is quite remarkable. With understanding we can strengthen relationships, revitalize neighborhoods, unify nations, and even bring peace to a troubled world. Without it chaos, intolerance, hate, and war are often the result.

In other words, *mis*understanding.

If I had to pick one word to describe my objective in writing this book, it would be *understanding.* More than anything else, I would like those who read these pages—especially those who are not members of The Church of Jesus Christ of Latter-day Saints—to better understand the Church and its members. That doesn't necessarily mean that my goal is to have every reader become a member of the Church, or even to accept our doctrines and practices—although I would be less than honest if I did not acknowledge that I would be pleased to see those things happen. But that isn't really the purpose of this book. This book is about comprehension and understanding, not conversion. It has more to do with building trust, appreciation, and respect than it does with increasing church membership.

And that understanding should begin with us—you, the

1

reader, and me. In order for you to understand me and my point of view a little better, you might want to know that I came into the world at about the same time as the Great Depression, which means that I grew up during a time when things were even tougher and more challenging economically than they are today. I watched my parents struggle to make ends meet, and I was affected by that. I attended public schools, went to college, met and married a wonderful woman, Barbara, who is the mother of our seven children. Professionally, my interests followed the real estate, investment, and automobile industries—including owning a dealership—until I was called in 1974 to serve as a full-time mission president and ecclesiastical leader of The Church of Jesus Christ of Latter-day Saints. Together as a family we've experienced good times and bad, success and failure; and we've known our share of both happiness and sadness.

What about you? Most likely we've never met, and yet I'm confident that we have a great deal in common. You are probably concerned about world events. You worry about conflict between nations and within individual countries, economic and social stability, and political turmoil. Perhaps you have dealt with serious illness, a reversal in fortune or unexpected disappointment, unemployment or the death of a loved one, and the pressure has taken its toll on you physically, spiritually, and emotionally. Your family is likely the most important thing in the world to you. Assuming that is the case, there are no doubt times when you look at the way things are going in the world and fear for the future of our children and grandchildren—in fact, for all of civilization as we know it.

So do I.

When it comes right down to it, people are quite similar. We may come from different backgrounds, cultures, and economic circumstances, and our attitudes and perspectives may vary. But in the heart—where it really counts—we're a lot alike.

An acquaintance of mine was visiting in the home of a business associate in another country. They had enjoyed a fine meal together and were sharing some pleasant conversation when the other man's teenage son burst into the room more than an hour after he was supposed to be home.

"I don't speak any language other than English," my friend told me while describing the experience, "but I was able to follow that short, tense conversation almost word-for-word: The father asked if the boy had any idea what time it was. The boy said he didn't know. The father asked if the boy remembered what time he was supposed to be home. The boy said he couldn't remember. The father asked where the boy had been. The boy said he'd been 'around.' The father asked why the boy had been so late. The boy said he lost track of time."

Finally the exasperated father dismissed the boy and turned his attention back to my friend. "I am so sorry," he said, and started to explain. But my friend stopped him.

"No explanation is necessary," my friend said. "I understand perfectly."

The man looked at my friend with a puzzled expression on his face. "I thought you didn't speak our language," he questioned.

"I don't," my friend told him. "But I do speak 'Parent.' And I've had that very conversation with my own teenagers at least a dozen times."

Such commonality should extend across all barriers—cultural, economic, and religious, to name just three—and bind us to one another despite our deepest differences. But that's not human nature, is it? Our tendency is to mistrust anything that departs from our own perception of normalcy, focusing so much attention on the things that divide us that

3

we lose track of the many things we hold in common that should unite us.

As a member of the Council of the Twelve Apostles and a General Authority, or a presiding minister and administrator, in The Church of Jesus Christ of Latter-day Saints (sometimes called the "Mormon" Church or the LDS Church), I think continually about religion and the impact it has on human relationships. The love that exists between people who share religious values and experiences can be the most satisfying and unifying force this side of the solid, happy family. At the same time, however, few things in life can be more potentially divisive than a different interpretation of religious truth. One needn't search far to find historical verification of that fact, or to find someone willing to provide a litany of the various atrocities committed by people in the name of religion. According to early American clergyman Samuel Davies, "Intolerance has been the curse of every age and state."

Curse or not, it's also true that those of us who are religiously active (including many members of The Church of Jesus Christ of Latter-day Saints) often create problems for ourselves by being overly enthusiastic about our faith. Sometimes we unwisely say things that can be misunderstood by neighbors and friends who belong to other churches. They may interpret this enthusiasm for our own beliefs as disrespect for theirs, which, instead of promoting understanding, may lead to defensiveness and dislike.

I understand how easily that can happen. Our missionaries knock on your door—uninvited—and ask to come into your home to share a gospel message. Your LDS neighbors talk about their church a lot—perhaps even more than your friends who belong to other faiths. They may have invited you to come to church with them or to listen to the missionaries in their home, and in their enthusiasm they may

4

have made a thoughtless remark about your beliefs or your lifestyle.

If you have ever had one or more of these experiences, I apologize. I am sure the offense was not intended. One of the most cherished tenets of our faith has to do with honoring religious diversity. As our church's first president, Joseph Smith, taught: "We claim the privilege of worshiping Almighty God according to the dictates of our own conscience, *and allow all men the same privilege, let them worship how, where, or what they may.*" (Article of Faith of The Church of Jesus Christ of Latter-day Saints, 11.)

We really do believe that. Just as we claim the right to worship as we choose, we believe you have the right to worship—or to not worship—as you see fit. All of our interpersonal relationships should be built on a foundation of mutual respect, trust, and appreciation. But that shouldn't prevent us from sharing deeply held religious feelings with each other. Indeed, we may find that our philosophical differences add flavor and perspective to our relationships, especially if those relationships are built on true values, openness, respect, trust, and understanding. *Especially* understanding.

Of course, I realize that life doesn't always work out the way it should. The subject of religion can be touchy, especially if it is handled insensitively. I heard about one member of our church, a father, who was moving his family into a new neighborhood. The man next door was outside watering his lawn. In an attempt to be neighborly, he shouted out an unassuming question: "Where do you folks come from?"

Our member knew an opening line when he heard it. He walked across his lawn, put a hand on the neighbor's shoulder, and responded, "What a profound question! Why don't you and your family come over to our house for dinner some night and we'll teach you the truth about where we

5

came from, why we're here, and where we're all going after this life is over."

It's easy to see how someone might be put off by such an approach. The sharing of religious feelings and beliefs is a deeply personal, even sacred thing. It can't be done very effectively in such a cavalier manner. Still, members of our church are constantly looking for opportunities to share the message of the restored gospel with friends, family members, neighbors, and anyone else who will listen.

Have you ever wondered why? Why are members of The Church of Jesus Christ of Latter-day Saints so anxious to talk about their religion, even with people who seem to be perfectly happy in their own churches and with their own way of life? Why don't we just focus our missionary efforts on the unchurched and the irreligious and leave the rest of the world alone? And what makes membership in our church such a consuming, motivating, inspiring passion anyway?

This book is an attempt to answer those questions honestly and directly with a simple declaration of what we believe to be true. I believe that this message is profoundly important, and that all of God's children—which includes all people everywhere—are entitled to hear it so they can decide for themselves if it has any validity for them and their families. My greatest hope is that by the time you reach the end of the book you will have a better *understanding*—there's that word again—of why we as a people feel such urgency in sharing our beliefs with others. And if it makes a positive difference in your life, even if only in your ability to understand and relate to your Mormon friends and family, so much the better.

Are you ready to begin? Let's start with a look at the central figure of our faith: the Lord Jesus Christ.

The Church
of Jesus Christ

The sun was about to set on another hectic Sunday in 1948 during my first mission for The Church of Jesus Christ of Latter-day Saints in Nottingham, England. I had just concluded a successful street meeting with other missionaries in the area, during which we shared our message with passersby on Nottingham Square.

"What makes you Americans think you can come here and teach us anything about Christianity?" one gentleman had asked.

It was a common question, and a legitimate one in my view. Unless we could offer people spiritual insights and understanding they couldn't receive anywhere else, there really wasn't much reason for them to listen to us. Thankfully, we had just such a message—one unique and laden with eternal significance—and I was pleased to be able to so testify to the gentleman who asked the question. We had a lively, interesting discussion, and I felt the spirit of the Lord with me as I taught the message of the gospel of Jesus Christ.

I was still feeling that same spirit at dusk as I walked home along the shores of the Trent River. It had been a long day, not discouraging but exhausting, filled with meetings and ministering which were associated with my assignment as a leader among the missionaries and members of the Church in Nottingham. I heard the soothing sounds of the river flowing downstream as I walked, my lungs filled with the dank, heavy air of England. I was thinking about the missionaries for whom I was responsible, as well as the Latter-day Saints in Nottingham who looked to me—a twenty-year-old American—as their leader. And I was thinking about that gentleman and the question he posed and the heartfelt testimony I presented in response.

As I strolled along the Trent, weary and yet happy and satisfied in the work, an overwhelming feeling of peace and understanding came over me. It was at that precise moment in time that I came to know that Jesus Christ knew me, that He loved me, and that He directed our missionary efforts. Of course I'd always believed those things. They were part of the testimony I had shared just a couple of hours earlier. But somehow in that instant of what I realized was pure revelation, my belief turned into knowledge. I didn't see any visions and I didn't hear any voices, but I could not have known of Christ's reality and divinity any more intensely had He stood before me and called out my name.

My life has been shaped by that experience. From that day to the present, every significant decision I have made has been influenced by my knowledge of the Savior. I couldn't, for example, entertain certain professional opportunities because they didn't represent the way Jesus would have done business. We have tried to base important family decisions on the Lord's will for us—whatever that may have been. Even personal relationships have been built on a foundation of love, our love for Christ and His love for us.

That's the way it is when Jesus Christ becomes a reality in your life. It isn't that He somehow makes you do things that you wouldn't do otherwise. Rather, you find yourself wanting to do what He would do and respond as He would respond in an effort to bring your life into harmony with

8

His. And an interesting thing happens whenever you attempt to place your feet in Christ's footsteps. If you really concentrate on trying to walk the way He walked—loving, caring, serving, and obeying each step of the way—one day you'll look up and discover that His path has led you directly to the throne of God. For that is and ever has been His great purpose and mission: to lead us to our Heavenly Father so we can dwell with Him in His heavenly home.

The Savior's Mission Didn't Begin in a Manger

As far as members of The Church of Jesus Christ of Latter-day Saints are concerned, the Savior's mission didn't begin in a manger-cradle in Bethlehem. It goes back much further than that, to a time when we all lived as the spirit children of our Heavenly Father. We didn't have physical bodies of flesh and bones as we now have, but the essence of our being—our spiritual selves, if you will—existed along with the rest of our Heavenly Father's spirit children.

Jesus was the greatest of these spirits. He was the first-born (Psalm 89:27), and He held a special place of honor with the Father "before the world was" (John 17:5). In that capacity He helped implement the plan that would bring us all to earth to obtain physical bodies and experience the vicissitudes of mortality so we could grow in our ability to obey God's commandments once we heard and understood them. Jesus, known in the Old Testament as Jehovah (for scriptural illumination on this significant concept please compare Isaiah 44:6 with Revelation 1:8; Isaiah 48:16 with John 8:56–58; and Isaiah 58:13–14 with Mark 2:28), even helped create the earth on which we live (see John 1:1–3 and Colossians 1:15–17); and as the second member of the Godhead comprised of the Father, the Son, and the Holy Ghost, He represented Heavenly Father in His dealings with early prophets and patriarchs.

When the time came for Jesus to be born, He was con-

9

ceived as "the only begotten of the Father." (John 1:14.)
Through His mother, Mary, he received many of the frailties
of mortality essential to His preordained and much-prophe-
sied mission to suffer and die for the sins of all mankind.
Through His Eternal Father He received certain powers of
immortality, which gave Him the ability to live a sinless life
and to eventually conquer death—for Himself and for us.

You may be familiar with the biblical account of Christ's
life and ministry. Your Latter-day Saint friends believe that
account in its entirety, as well as some additional information that can be found in the Book of Mormon: Another Testament of Jesus Christ. We'll speak of the Book of Mormon
in more detail later, but for now I'll just quote from its title
page, which informs readers that one of the main reasons
for the preservation of this book of scripture is "to the con-
vincing of the Jew and Gentile that Jesus is the Christ, the
Eternal God, manifesting himself unto all nations."

That Jesus Christ would be the focal point of worship
by Christians everywhere is in itself something of a miracle. After all, the Savior's earthly mission was a short one.
He lived in mortality but thirty-three years, and His active
ecclesiastical ministry stretched across just three years. But
in that three-year period He taught the human family everything we must know in order to receive all of the blessings
our Father in Heaven has promised us, His children. By
virtue of His faith and authority the Savior performed
mighty miracles, from changing water into wine at a wedding feast in Cana to raising His friend Lazarus from the
dead. And He concluded His mortal ministry with the single most incredible accomplishment in the history of the
world: the Atonement.

The Atonement: The Most Heroic Act of All Time

It is impossible to put into words the full meaning of the
atonement of Christ. Entire volumes have been written on

10

this subject. But for our purposes here, let me try to explain in brief, simple terms what the atonement of Jesus Christ means to me—and what it could mean to you.

I remember reading about a fire fighter in the eastern United States who ran into a burning house to rescue several children from an arson-induced fire. While his colleagues battled the blaze to keep it from spreading to other structures in the neighborhood, this man dashed into the building again and again, each time emerging with a child in his arms. After rescuing the fifth child, he started back into the inferno once more. Neighbors shouted that there were no more children in the family. But he insisted that he had seen a baby in a cradle, and he dove into the intensifying heat.

Moments after he disappeared into the fire and smoke, a horrifying explosion shook the building and the entire structure collapsed. It was several hours before fire fighters were able to locate their colleague's body. They found him in the nursery near the crib, huddled protectively over a life-sized—and practically unscratched—doll.

I'm overwhelmed by that story. I'm touched by the fire fighter's courageous and selfless devotion to duty, and I'm thankful that there are men and women in the world who are willing to put their lives on the line for the sake of others.

As I think about such heroism, however, I'm reminded that the most heroic act of all time ever was performed in behalf of all mankind by the Son of God. In a very real sense, all of humanity—past, present, and future—was trapped behind a wall of flame that was fueled and fanned by our own faithlessness. Sin separated mortals from God (see Romans 6:23), and would do so forever unless a way was found to put out the fires of sin and rescue us from ourselves. The way would not be easy, for it required the vicarious sacrifice of One who was sinless and who was willing to pay the price of sin for all of humanity, now and forever.

11

Thankfully, that most significant role was heroically played by Jesus Christ on two different stages in ancient Jerusalem. The first act was performed quietly, on bended knee in the Garden of Gethsemane. There in the quiet isolation of gnarled olive trees and sturdy boulders, and in some incredible way that none of us can fully comprehend, the Savior took upon Himself the sins of the world. Even though His life was pure and free of sin, He paid the ultimate penalty for sin—yours, mine, and the sins of everyone who ever lived. His mental and emotional anguish were so great that it caused Him to bleed from every pore (see Luke 22:44). And yet He did it, willingly, so that we might all have the cleansing opportunity of repentance through faith in Jesus Christ, without which none of us would be worthy of entrance into God's kingdom.

The second act was performed just hours later in the torture chambers of Jerusalem and on the cross at Calvary, where He endured the agony of inquisition, cruel beatings, and death by crucifixion. The Savior didn't have to go through that. As the Son of God, He had the power to alter the situation in any number of ways. Yet He allowed Himself to be battered and abused, humiliated and executed, so that we could receive the priceless gift of immortality. The atonement of Jesus Christ was an awful yet indispensable part of Heavenly Father's plan for His Son's earthly mission. Because Jesus died and then conquered death through His resurrection, all of us will have the privilege of immortality. This gift is given freely through the loving grace of Jesus Christ to all people of all ages, regardless of their good or evil acts. And to those who choose to love the Lord and who show their love and faith in Him by keeping His commandments, the Atonement offers the additional promise of exaltation, or the privilege of living in the presence of God forever.

Members of The Church of Jesus Christ of Latter-day

Saints often sing a hymn, "I Stand All Amazed," that expresses what I feel when I consider the Savior's benevolent atoning sacrifice:

> *I stand all amazed at the love Jesus*
> *   offers me,*
> *Confused at the grace that so fully he*
> *   proffers me.*
> *I tremble to know that for me he was*
> *   crucified,*
> *That for me, a sinner, he suffered, he*
> *   bled and died.*
>
> *Oh, it is wonderful*
> *that he should care for me*
> *Enough to die for me!*
> *Oh, it is wonderful,*
> *Wonderful to me!*

The Living Christ and the Cross

With all of this feeling among Mormons for Jesus Christ and His marvelous atonement, you may have wondered why you've never seen your LDS neighbors wearing a cross on a necklace, or why there are no crosses adorning LDS buildings or literature. Most other Christians use the cross as a symbol of their devotion to Christ, a physical reminder of His crucifixion on Calvary. So why don't members of The Church of Jesus Christ of Latter-day Saints follow suit?

We revere Jesus. He is the Head of our Church, which bears His name. He is our Savior and our Redeemer. We love Him. Through Him we worship and pray to our Heavenly Father. We are grateful beyond measure for the essential and awesome power His atonement has in each of our lives.

But while thoughts of the blood He shed for us in Gethsemane and on Calvary fill our hearts with profound appreciation, it isn't just the fact that He died that is so meaningful to us. Our hope and faith are rooted in the profound understanding that He lives today, and that He continues to lead and guide His Church and His people through His spirit. We rejoice in the knowledge of a living Christ, and we reverently acknowledge the miracles He continues to work today in the lives of those who have faith in Him. That is why we choose to place less emphasis on a symbol that can be construed to represent primarily His death.

Living a Christ-Centered Life

We believe that only as we focus our attention on the Savior and build our lives upon the strong foundation the Atonement and gospel give us, are we prepared to resist the challenges and temptations so prevalent in today's world.

A Book of Mormon prophet named Nephi explained it this way:

"Wherefore, ye must press forward with a steadfastness in Christ, having a perfect brightness of hope, and a love of God and of all men. Wherefore, if ye shall press forward, feasting upon the word of Christ, and endure to the end, behold, thus saith the Father: Ye shall have eternal life.

"And now . . . this is the way; and there is none other way nor name given under heaven whereby man can be saved in the kingdom of God." (2 Nephi 31:20–21.)

This is why our belief in Christ is not passive. We believe that He and our Heavenly Father continue to minister to mankind today through inspiration and revelation. The leaders of The Church of Jesus Christ of Latter-day Saints function under His divine direction just as the early apostles and prophets did when His Church was fully upon the earth. Ours is an active, vibrant faith dedicated to serving the Lord and doing the things He would do if He were walking

14

among us. As we do His will we feel His spirit, a peaceful, comforting presence that warms our souls with courage and faith and draws us ever closer to Him. And as we draw closer to Him, we learn to love Him and our Eternal Father, and we find ourselves showing our love for them by keeping their commandments—which helps us to become more like them.

Focus on the Prince of Peace

Not that we can ever really become just like Jesus. But as we commit ourselves to Him—spiritually, physically, and emotionally—He blesses our lives with loving direction. Every decision we make from that time on is affected, because there are certain things a man or woman of Christ simply will not do. Our actions become more disciplined, our relationships become more righteous; even our language becomes more pure as we live a life that is centered on Jesus Christ and His teachings. Simply put, after the spirit of Christ enters our hearts and our souls, we can never be the same again.

That doesn't mean we suddenly become perfect. We all fall short of that mark, which is why we're so thankful for the gift of repentance through our faith in Christ. It just means that we're always trying to live up to the responsibility of being a true follower of Christ, not because we fear Him or Heavenly Father but because we love them and want to serve them.

The best thing about living a Christ-centered life, however, is how it makes you feel—inside. It's hard to have a negative attitude about things if and when your life is focused on the Prince of Peace. There will still be problems. Everyone has them. But faith in the Lord Jesus Christ is a power to be reckoned with in the universe and in individual lives. It can be a causative force through which miracles are wrought. It can also be a source of inner strength through

15

which we find self-esteem, peace of mind, contentment, and the courage to cope. I have seen marriages saved, families strengthened, tragedies overcome, careers energized, and the will to go on living rekindled as people humble themselves before the Lord and accept His will in their lives. Heartache, tragedy, and trauma of all kinds can be focused and managed when the principles of the gospel of Jesus Christ are understood and applied.

Nothing in Life Works Until . . .

Take Jeff and Kimberly, for example, both fine young people—attractive, intelligent, and personable. Everyone who knew them thought their marriage would be ideal. And it was—for a few months. But then they started to drift apart as Jeff focused more and more attention on his schooling and sports activities, while Kimberly found herself consumed by her work. There was little to hold them together, nothing to unite them in spirit and purpose. By the time their first anniversary rolled around, they were both thinking about writing off the marriage as an unfortunate mistake.

Less than two years later, however, their marriage was solid and secure. Their secret? They found their commonality in Christ.

"We tried everything we could think of," Kimberly said. "But nothing really worked until we decided to go back to church. It was there that we started feeling familiar spiritual yearnings that bound us together as we sought the Lord's will in our lives. When we knelt together in prayer again, asking Heavenly Father to bless and help us, everything came back into focus and our love and respect for each other increased."

That focus was also a problem for Steven—only more so. Confused and muddled by counter-culture philosophies of the sixties, Steven found himself in the mid-1970s drifting across America, aimlessly looking for meaning and direction in his life. He was drifting through San Diego when he met two Mormon missionaries.

"Hey!" he shouted as they bicycled past him in a quiet residential neighborhood. "You guys selling anything good?"

The missionaries glanced in his direction, and, to be perfectly candid, were inclined to ignore his question and peddle on. If ever there was an unlikely looking prospect for their message, it was Steven. He had shoulder-length hair and a thick, unkempt beard, and was wearing tattered jeans, a T-shirt, sandals, and a captain's hat. His face and hands were dirty and an unlit cigarette dangled precariously from his mouth.

The missionaries looked at each other. Then at Steven. Then at each other again.

"We're not selling anything," one missionary said with a shrug and a smile. "What we have we're giving away."

"Okay," Steven said. "I'll take whatever it is you're giving away."

The missionaries laughed. Steven laughed. And then they started to talk. Somehow during that conversation the missionaries sensed the depth of Steven's spiritual longing. He invited them to his small, cluttered apartment, where they began to teach him about Jesus Christ and His supreme role in God's eternal plan for His children. After a two-hour discussion, the missionaries set up another appointment with Steven for the next day.

It wouldn't have surprised either missionary if Steven hadn't been in his apartment at the appointed hour. But there he was. Only there was something different about him. His eyes were bright and clear, and he and his room were clean.

"Right after you left yesterday I took a shower, cleaned

up the place, and dumped out my booze," Steven announced. "It just seemed like the thing to do."

The missionaries were stunned. But not as stunned as they were the next day, when they arrived for their third meeting with Steven and found that he had trimmed his hair and beard.

Once again he explained by saying, "It just seemed like the thing to do."

So did purchasing some clean clothes. And getting a job. And terminating his association with certain groups of friends. Every day the missionaries arrived to find that Steven had chosen to make significant changes in his life and lifestyle. The missionaries were teaching him about Jesus Christ and His gospel, but they hadn't asked him to make any changes yet. Steven just went ahead and made them—willingly and completely—because the spirit of Christ was making a difference in his life by making a difference in him. Today this spiritual vagabond is a devoted family man, a successful businessman, and a faithful disciple of the Lord Jesus Christ.

Coming unto Christ

In one of the scriptural records that comprise the Book of Mormon, a great spiritual leader named Helaman counseled his sons to "remember that it is upon the rock of our Redeemer, who is Christ, the Son of God, that ye must build your foundation; that when the devil shall send forth his mighty winds, yea, his shafts in the whirlwind, yea, when all his hail and his mighty storm shall beat upon you, it shall have no power over you to drag you down to the gulf of misery and endless wo, because of the rock upon which ye are built, which is a sure foundation, a foundation whereon if men build they cannot fall." (Helaman 5:12.)

My grandfather understood that concept. Even though he died when I was just ten years old, Melvin J. Ballard has been a major influence in my life. For as long as I can remember I have heard my family talk about his love for the Lord and his unwavering devotion to the Church. He spent his entire life building on the "sure foundation" of which Helaman spoke, and I'm not aware of any "shafts in the whirlwind" that were able to penetrate his faith and testimony. In fact, my personal quest for knowledge of the Savior was motivated to a great degree by Grandfather Ballard's account of one of his most sacred experiences.

While he was serving a mission among American Indians in the Northwest, my grandfather faced a time of incredible struggle. There were unprecedented—and seemingly insurmountable—challenges for the Church there, and my grandfather literally spent hours on his knees asking for guidance and inspiration. During one such period, when all seemed bleak and utterly hopeless, grandfather received, in his words, "a wonderful manifestation and impression which has never left me.

A Witness That He Lives

"I was told there was a [great] privilege that was to be mine," he recorded. "I was led into a room where I was informed I was to meet someone. As I entered the room I saw, seated on a raised platform, the most glorious being I have ever conceived of, and was taken forward to be introduced to Him. As I approached He smiled, called my name, and stretched out His hands toward me. If I live to be a million years old I shall never forget that smile.

"He put His arms around me and kissed me, as He took me into His bosom, and He blessed me until my whole being was thrilled. As He finished I fell at His feet, and there saw the marks of the nails; and as I kissed them, with deep joy swelling through my whole being, I felt that I was in heaven indeed.

"The feeling that came to my heart then was: Oh! if I

could live worthy, though it would require four-score years, so that in the end when I have finished I could go into His presence and receive the feeling that I *then* had in His presence, I would give everything that I am and ever hope to be!"

Grandfather concluded: "I know—as I know that I live— that *He* lives. That is my testimony." (*Melvin J. Ballard— Crusader for Righteousness*, Salt Lake City: Bookcraft, 1966.)

That experience infused my grandfather with the comfort, determination, and spiritual energy he needed to deal with the problems he was encountering on his mission. In fact, the day after he received that manifestation, he joined one of his fellow missionaries, W. Leo Isgren, in visiting a well-to-do merchant in Helena, Montana. Some years later, Brother Isgren told me how he and my grandfather had stood together in front of a life-sized portrait of Jesus Christ that was prominently displayed in the merchant's home. At length, grandfather turned to Brother Isgren.

"No, that isn't Him," grandfather said. "The artist has made a fair representation of Him, but that isn't Him."

"I was filled so much with a sacred feeling that I could say nothing," Brother Isgren told me. "After we left the home and were on our way to our next appointment, Brother Ballard stopped me and said, 'Brother Isgren, I suppose you were somewhat startled at my words regarding the Savior of the world.' I told him that, yes, indeed, I had been—very much so. And then and there firsthand he told me of his experience the previous evening."

While we may not all have experiences of that same magnitude or intensity, the essence of our ministry in The Church of Jesus Christ of Latter-day Saints is to invite all people everywhere to "come unto Christ" so that He can work His miracle in their lives in whatever way He chooses. For some, that miracle will mean a significant change of life and lifestyle. For others it will simply mean new purpose and understanding in lives that are already rich with faith. But for all it will mean peace and joy and happiness beyond measure as the Master touches hearts and souls with His love. That's what my Grandfather Ballard felt as a result of his dramatic manifestation, and that's what I felt in a quieter, calmer way that evening near the Trent River in Nottingham, England.

That testimony has been with me ever since. It has sustained me through trials, comforted me in times of need, and given me a clear direction to follow whenever I have been confused or discouraged. Through my service as one of His Apostles I have had many special spiritual experiences that confirm and secure my personal knowledge of Him as the Savior and Redeemer of the children of God. Because I know that Jesus Christ lives and that He loves me, I find the courage to repent and to strive to be what He would want me to be. I know this knowledge can do the same for you, if you want it to—now, and forever.

Falling Away

CHAPTER TWO

"President, guess what?"

The voice on the telephone was familiar—and exuberant. It was one of the missionaries I was supervising during my service as president of the Church's mission in Toronto, Ontario, Canada. I had come to love each one of the dedicated men and women (referred to during the term of their service as "elders" and "sisters") who had made the commitment to serve the Lord as missionaries. But I had also come to expect the unexpected, especially from energetic young men and women.

"I just can't guess, Elder," I replied, somewhat apprehensively. "I've had so many surprises since I've been here that I won't even try."

He cleared his throat, then he proclaimed: "My companion and I have made an appointment for you to speak at the School of Theology at Toronto University!"

From the sound of his voice it was clear that my young friend expected I would greet his announcement with the kind of unbridled excitement usually reserved for championship sporting events. Experience, however, had taught me to keep a tight reign on my enthusiasm at such times.

"Well, that's very interesting," I responded carefully. "But what does it mean?"

He paused a moment, during which I heard him speaking in hushed, anxious tones with his missionary companion. "We aren't really sure," he said with a little less conviction in his voice. "We think it means that you're going to teach a group of ministers from other religions why our church is true!"

I couldn't help but chuckle, and not just because of his innocent bravado. Our conversation triggered the memory of a time some twenty-seven years earlier when I had arranged a similar "opportunity" for my mission president in England. I even toyed with the idea of responding the same way my mission president had responded to me: he left it to me to personally fulfill the assignment I had arranged for him of speaking before the Midland Debating Society in Nottingham.

But the prospect of sharing my beliefs with a group of ministers was intriguing, so I chose to accept this invitation. On the appointed day I traveled to the School of Theology in Toronto and met with about forty-five ministers, who were all seated around a large table. I was given forty-five minutes to explain the basic teachings of the Church, then the ministers were free to ask questions.

The first comment, issued in the form of a challenge, was, "Mr. Ballard, if you could just place the Gold Plates from which the Book of Mormon was translated on this table so all of us could handle them, then we would know that what you are telling us is the truth."

I felt prompted to respond by looking the questioner in the eye and saying, "You are a minister, and you know that no truth has ever come into the heart of man except by the Holy Ghost. You could hold the Gold Plates in your hands, and you would not know any more about whether this Church is true than before. May I ask, have you read the Book of Mormon?"

He answered that he had not.

I replied, "Don't you believe it would be wise to read the Book of Mormon, and then ponder and pray and ask God if the Book of Mormon is true?"

The second question came from a Protestant minister: "Mr. Ballard, do you mean to tell us that unless we are baptized into the Mormon Church we will not be saved in heaven?"

That is a difficult question to answer when speaking to forty-five ministers from other churches. But the Spirit of the Lord moved quickly to help me form a response.

"Well, the safest way to answer that question would be to say that we're very thankful a kind and loving Father in Heaven will be the one to determine who will and will not be admitted into His kingdom, and then just let it go at that," I said. "But that isn't what you're really asking, is it?"

The minister agreed that his question went much deeper.

"Let me see if I can cut to the heart of your question this way," I continued. "We believe that truth can be found wherever people sincerely seek it, and we believe there are many sincere and wonderful people in every religious denomination. But I must tell you with all due respect that only The Church of Jesus Christ of Latter-day Saints teaches the fullness of the gospel of Jesus Christ. Therefore, we do not believe the leadership of any other church has God's full authority to act in His name to perform a baptism or any other sacred ordinance. We love all people as our brothers and sisters, and we believe we are all the spirit children of the same Heavenly Father. But it would be wrong if I didn't humbly submit to you that whatever ecclesiastical authority you have, it is incomplete."

A heavy silence filled the room. I didn't expect that this group would take kindly to such a suggestion from me, but any other response would have been dishonest on my part. Please don't misunderstand: I am inspired by the wonderful things being done by my learned and committed colleagues from other faith groups all around the world. These are noble men and women who have dedicated their lives to their faith, and the world is a better place because of them. They bring comfort to the sick, peace to the troubled, and hope to the weary and downtrodden. I am convinced that God works through them to bless the lives of His children in remarkable ways.

But there is order in God's kingdom, an order that can only be administered through Heavenly Father's duly designated priesthood authority. And as much as I admire and appreciate the ministry of esteemed clerics the world over, I must boldly proclaim now as I did to those Canadian ministers to whom I was speaking that God's *full* authority can only be found in The Church of Jesus Christ of Latter-day Saints.

Priesthood Authority Was Lost for Centuries

I realize that that is quite a claim, especially when we consider all of the other religious organizations that profess similar authority. And many of those organizations have been around much longer than our church. How can we claim Heavenly Father's full authority when others can trace their ecclesiastical roots back through the Middle Ages to the time of Christ Himself? Quite simply, The Church of Jesus Christ of Latter-day Saints teaches that God's full authority was lost from the earth for centuries following the mortal ministry of the Lord Jesus Christ and His Apostles, and that full authority wasn't restored until it was given through marvelous manifestation to a nineteenth-century prophet named Joseph Smith.

We'll speak more of the restoration of the gospel later. But first we need to address the most basic question: Did Christ's authority need to be restored? After all, if the Church He organized and its attendant priesthood authority survived through the ages, Joseph Smith's claims would have no factual basis.

Some people are surprised to learn that Jesus Christ actually organized a church during His comparatively brief life on earth. But scriptural evidence is abundantly clear on the matter. The New Testament tells us that the Lord organized a quorum of twelve apostles. He laid His hands upon them and conferred the authority to act in His name. The Apostle Paul taught that Christ "gave some, apostles; and some, prophets; and some, evangelists; and some, pastors and teachers;

"For the perfecting of the saints, for the work of the ministry, for the edifying of the body of Christ;

"Till we all come in the unity of the faith, and of the knowledge of the Son of God, unto a perfect man, unto the measure of the stature of the fulness of Christ:

"That we henceforth be no more children, tossed to and fro, and carried about with every wind of doctrine, by the sleight of men, and cunning craftiness, whereby they lie in wait to deceive." (Ephesians 4:11–14.)

It is commonly understood that after the death, resurrection, and ascension of Christ, Peter became the chief apostle, or president of the Lord's Church. This wasn't an easy task in those days. In addition to the challenges of persecution and hardship endured by early Christians, Peter and his brethren had a difficult time holding the Church together and keeping the doctrine pure. They traveled a great deal and wrote to one another frequently about the problems they were facing. But information moved so slowly, travel was so laborious, and the Church and its teachings were so new that it was difficult to head off false doctrine and teachings before they became firmly entrenched.

"I marvel that ye are so soon removed from him that called you into the grace of Christ unto another gospel," Paul wrote to the churches of Galatia. "Which is not another;

but there be some that trouble you, and would pervert the gospel of Christ.

"But though we, or an angel from heaven, preach any other gospel unto you than that which we have preached unto you, let him be accursed.

"As we said before, so say I now again, If any man preach any other gospel unto you than that ye have received, let him be accursed.

"For do I now persuade men, or God? or do I seek to please men? for if I yet pleased men, I should not be the servant of Christ." (Galatians 1:6–10.)

The scriptures indicate that although the early apostles worked hard to preserve the Church that Jesus Christ left to their care and keeping, they knew their efforts would eventually be consumed by crisis. Paul wrote the Thessalonian Christians who were anxiously anticipating the Second Coming of Christ that "that day shall not come, except there come a falling away first, and that man of sin be revealed, the son of perdition." (2 Thessalonians 2:3.) He also warned Timothy that "the time will come when they will not endure sound doctrine; but after their own lusts shall they heap to themselves teachers, having itching ears; And they shall turn away their ears from the truth, and shall be turned unto fables." (2 Timothy 4:3–4.) And Peter presupposed an apostasy when he spoke of the "times of refreshing" that would come before God would again send Jesus Christ, "which before was preached unto you: Whom the heaven must receive until the times of restitution of all things, which God hath spoken by the mouth of all his holy prophets since the world began." (Acts 3:20–21.)

The Priesthood Is God's Authority on Earth

Eventually Peter was slain by his enemies. It is believed that he was martyred sometime between A.D. 60 and 70. After Peter's death, the remaining apostles and their faithful

28

followers struggled for survival in the face of horrifying oppression. To their everlasting credit, Christianity was preserved, and by the end of the second century A.D. it was truly a force to be reckoned with. Linus, Cletus, Clement, and other bishops of Rome were instrumental in helping Christianity endure. Were it not for these faithful saints, the good news of Christ's ministry might have been lost altogether.

There are those who believe that Peter's successor as president of the Church that Christ organized was Linus. In A.D. 79 Cletus succeeded Linus, and then Clement became bishop of Rome and the next successor in A.D. 90.

But the important question is, Was apostolic power transferred from Peter to Linus?

It is significant to note that not all of the original Twelve Apostles had died by this time. John the Beloved, for example, was exiled to the Isle of Patmos. While there, John received the Book of Revelation—a standard book in all Christian Bibles—which raises an interesting and fundamentally crucial question: If Linus was head of the Church, and if he succeeded Peter, why wasn't the Book of Revelation revealed through him? Why did it come through John, an Apostle in exile?

The answer is clear. The revelation came through John because he was the last living Apostle, the last man holding the keys and authority, as designated by the Savior Himself, of Apostleship. When God spoke to the Church, He therefore did so through His Apostle, John, on the Isle of Patmos. We do not believe the Lord would have bypassed John, who clearly had apostolic power, when speaking to the Church.

As significant as the individual ministries of Linus, Cletus, and Clement doubtless were, there is no evidence to suggest that these men continued to function as an authoritative Council of Twelve Apostles—the administrative body that the Lord placed at the head of the earthly church He Himself organized. Without the authority and direction of the Council of Twelve Apostles, men began looking to other sources for doctrinal understanding, and as a result many plain and precious truths were lost.

History tells us, for example, of a great council held in A.D. 325 in Nicaea in Bithyria, Asia Minor. By this time Christianity had emerged from the dank dungeons of Rome to become the state religion of the Roman Empire. But there were still problems—chiefly the inability of Christians to agree among themselves on basic points of doctrine. So great was the strife created by these dogmatic disputes that Emperor Constantine called together a group of Christian bishops to establish the official doctrines of the Church— and, not coincidentally, to achieve greater political unity within the empire.

It wasn't easy. Opinions on such basic subjects as the nature of God were diverse and deeply felt, and debate was spirited and chaotic. This council defined God as a spirit who had universal power and yet was so small he could dwell in one's heart. Out of this council came the Nicene Creed. Decisions were made by majority vote, and some disagreeing factions split off and formed new churches. Similar doctrinal councils were later held at Chalcedon (A.D. 451), Nicaea (A.D. 787), and Trent (A.D. 1545), with similarly divisive results each time. The beautiful simplicity of Christ's gospel was under attack from an enemy even more destructive than the scourges and crosses of early Rome: the philosophical meanderings of learned-but-uninspired men, which resulted in doctrine based more on popular opinion than revelation.

It's no wonder, then, that the thousand-year period known as the Middle Ages wasn't exactly the best of times for Christianity. The name of the Lord was invoked upon all manner of horrifying campaigns, from the Crusades to the Inquisition, leaving a bloody trail of death, persecution, and destruction. Christ's central teachings of faith, hope, charity, and tolerance seemed lost upon zealots who were absolutely determined that "every knee shall bow," one way or another.

While there continued to be Christians who believed basically in the message of Jesus Christ, over time the doctrines became distorted and the authority to act in the name of God—in other words, the priesthood—disappeared. After a period of years, the Apostles died who had received their priesthood, their spiritual assignment, and their ordination in the time of Christ. They took their priesthood authority with them. In short, the church Christ organized gradually disintegrated, and the fulness of the gospel was lost.

These were indeed Dark Ages. The light of the *fulness* of the gospel of Jesus Christ, including the authority of His holy priesthood, was gone.

The Reformation

But in 1517 the spirit of Christ moved upon a Catholic priest living in Germany. Martin Luther was among a growing number of thoughtful clergymen who were disturbed by how far the church had strayed from the gospel as taught by Christ. Luther created a good deal of controversy when he publicly called for reformation by posting on his church door a list of items and issues that he felt needed to be debated.

Although John Wycliffe and others had called for a return to New Testament Christianity nearly a century earlier, it was Luther who launched the Protestant movement—although it should be noted that his followers, not Luther himself, actually organized the Lutheran Church. Soon other visionaries such as John Calvin, Huldrych Zwingli, John Wesley, and John Smith took up the movement. These men gave rise to religious orders that broke new theological ground while continuing certain aspects of the Catholic tradition from which they sprang.

The Inspired Reformers

I believe that these great reformers were inspired by God. They helped to prepare the world for the restoration of the fulness of the gospel through the Prophet Joseph Smith in 1820 by creating a religious climate that allowed for difference. Because of the religious intolerance that existed in the world, I doubt that the gospel of Jesus Christ could have been restored even one century earlier. And can you imagine what might have happened during the Inquisition if someone outside the religious mainstream had claimed revelation from God?

That's why I believe the reformers played an important role in preparing the world for the Restoration. So did the early explorers and colonizers of America and the framers of the Constitution of the United States. God needed a philosophical climate that allowed for theological restoration and a political arena where people could share ideas and talk about their beliefs openly without fear of persecution or death. He created such a place on the American continent—thanks to those reformers, explorers, and patriots—and by the early 1800s the American frontier fairly bristled with interdenominational fervor and excitement. Ministers competed for the hearts and souls of entire congregations. Cities, towns, and even families were divided by their various religious alliances. Never in the history of the world did the sincere seeker of truth have more ecclesiastical options from which to choose.

Clearly the world was ripe for the "restitution of all things" spoken of by Peter and "all [God's] holy prophets since the world began." (Acts 3:20–21.)

Because of the Apostasy, the priesthood and authority and power to act in the name of God had to be restored to the earth.

The Restoration

By the year 1820, religious fervor was sweeping across the American countryside. It was as though the Protestant reformation that had blossomed in Europe several centuries earlier had finally reached full bloom in Palmyra, a sleepy village in upstate New York. Ministers from different denominations vied for the loyalty of the faithful. Lay members zealously defended the correctness of their personal religious preferences. Itinerant preachers held revival meetings on the outskirts of town, each with his own unique style and message.

For the family of Joseph and Lucy Mack Smith, such religious excitement was especially intriguing. The family's roots ran deep in America's spiritual history. In 1638 Robert Smith left England for the promised religious freedom of colonial America. More than a century later his grandson, Samuel Smith, Jr., fought to preserve that and other cherished freedoms as a captain in George Washington's revolutionary army. One of Captain Smith's soldiers was his son, Asael, who once recorded that "it has been born in upon my soul that one of my descendants will promulgate a work to revolutionize the world of religious thought." (George Albert Smith, "History of George Albert Smith," Historical

Department of The Church of Jesus Christ of Latter-day Saints, Salt Lake City, Utah.)

Which Church to Join?

Asael's son, Joseph, was well aware of his rich spiritual heritage. He and his wife, Lucy, were deeply devoted to God, and their children were well schooled in the principles of faith and righteousness. Even so, the family became something of a microcosm of the division among the different churches in Palmyra. Mother Smith and three of her children—Hyrum, Samuel, and Sophronia—joined the Presbyterian Church, while Father Smith and his eldest son, Alvin, affiliated with the Methodists. There is no record that this variance caused contention in the Smith home, but it seems likely that the situation was a topic of lively discussion among family members from time to time.

When the time came for Joseph and Lucy's fourteen-year-old son Joseph, Jr. to be baptized, he had to decide which church to join, and he investigated each denomination carefully. A serious, thoughtful boy with a profound spiritual nature, he listened to the respective ministers and sorted out the truth as best he could. At first he was inclined to follow his father and Alvin into the Methodist Church. But then he would hear the Presbyterian minister attack the Methodists, and his confidence in the Methodist faith wavered. Then the Baptist minister would convince him that the Presbyterian minister was in error. And then a revivalist preacher would visit and persuade him that everyone—except himself—was wrong.

Imagine the Smith family, sitting around the dinner table at the end of a long day's work. Mother Lucy is seated at one end of the table, with Father Joseph at the other end and the children seated in between. As is so often the case, the conversation turns to the subject of religion. In our imaginary discussion, young Joseph has indicated that he wants

to be baptized, but he can't decide who should do the baptizing.

"Jesus was baptized," Joseph may have reasoned, "so that means I need to be baptized, too. Mother's minister has invited me to be baptized at his church. But Father's minister says that I won't go to heaven if I'm baptized as a Presbyterian. Then the Baptist minister tells me that he's the only one in town who knows anything about baptism. And now I don't know what to do. Can I just let them all take turns baptizing me? Or do I have to pick one of them? And if I do, which one should I pick?"

While that may not be exactly how it happened, the depth and sincerity of young Joseph Smith's questions were real. This was an extraordinary young man raised in an extraordinary family during extraordinary times. His motives were honest and his heart was pure. Though he was still but a lad—or perhaps because of it—he was open and receptive to the spirit of the Lord, and he was prepared and willing to respond to it.

Heavenly Father and Jesus Christ Visit Joseph Smith

"In the midst of this war of words and tumult of opinion," Joseph Smith later wrote in his own historical account of his experience, "I often said to myself, What is to be done? Who, of all these parties, are right? Or are they all wrong together? If any of them be right, which is it, and how shall I know it?"

Joseph looked for answers to his questions in the scriptures, but sometimes all he found were more questions. Perhaps he read the Savior's promise to His disciples that "ye shall know the truth, and the truth shall make you free" (John 8:32) and wondered when he would experience that glorious freedom. And perhaps he read Paul's teaching that "there is one body, and one Spirit. . . . One Lord, one faith, one baptism" (Ephesians 4:4–5) and asked himself, "But which one is the one?"

Then came the day that forever changed the course of life for young Joseph and the entire Smith family—not to mention the lives of millions of others around the world.

Joseph was reading in the Bible when he came upon a simple, direct admonition in the general epistle of James: "If any of you lack wisdom, let him ask of God, that giveth to all men liberally, and upbraideth not; and it shall be given him." (James 1:5.)

"Never did any passage of scripture come with more power to the heart of man than this did at this time to mine," Joseph wrote. "It seemed to enter with great force into every feeling of my heart. I reflected on it again and again, knowing that if any person needed wisdom from God, I did; for how to act I did not know, and unless I could get more wisdom than I then had, I would never know." (Joseph Smith–History 1:12.)

With the simple faith of one just past childhood and motivated by the inspiration of the scriptures and the Holy Spirit, Joseph decided to go into the woods near his home and put James's promise to the test.

Although it was a beautiful spring morning, Joseph was probably more focused on his errand than his surroundings as he made his way deeper and deeper into the woods. It was the first time it had occurred to him to make the subject of his confusion and religious distress a matter of personal prayer, and he spent considerable time forming in his mind the words he would speak. So great was his faith in God's power to fulfill James's scriptural promise that, I believe, he fully expected to receive an answer to his question.

What he received, however, went so far beyond that as to defy comprehension.

Joseph paused when he arrived at the quiet, secluded spot in the woods he had selected for this special moment.

He looked around to make sure he was alone, then knelt and began to pray. Immediately an overwhelming feeling of dangerous darkness swept over him, as if some evil power were trying to dissuade him from his determination. Rather than surrender to the fear, Joseph intensified his pleas to God.

At the very moment that he felt as though he would "sink into despair and abandon [himself] to destruction," God Himself responded.

"I saw a pillar of light exactly over my head, above the brightness of the sun, which descended gradually until it fell upon me," Joseph later recorded. "When the light rested upon me, I saw two Personages, whose brightness and glory defy all description, standing above me in the air. One of them spake unto me, calling me by name and said, pointing to the other, *This is my beloved Son. Hear Him!*" (JS–H 1:16–17.)

It was God, our Heavenly Father, appearing with His Resurrected Son, Jesus Christ—clearly one of the most magnificent spiritual manifestations of all time!

But according to his account of the event, Joseph didn't pause to consider the historical implications of what he was experiencing. He was simply a teenage boy in need of spiritual guidance, and so he asked the question he had intended to ask: "Which of all the sects is right, and which should I join?"

He was told that he should join none of the churches, that the pure doctrines of the gospel had become distorted during the centuries that had passed since the death and resurrection of Jesus Christ. And then, their mission accomplished, the Father and His Son, Jesus Christ, departed, leaving young Joseph physically drained but spiritually enriched.

It was some time before Joseph found the strength to

make his way back home. As soon as she saw him, his mother could tell that something was troubling her son.

"Never mind, all is well—I am well enough off," he responded to her inquiries. Then he added: "I have learned for myself that Presbyterianism is not true."

Eventually Joseph Smith shared his experience with others. To their everlasting credit, his spiritually sensitive family knew that he was telling the truth, and they supported his every claim from the very beginning. The entire family had been prepared to assume a meaningful role in the restoration of the gospel through their son and brother, and they responded accordingly.

Others, however, were skeptical and, on occasion, even violent. So intense was the persecution from many who heard his story that Joseph must have been tempted to deny the report, or to at least pretend it had never happened.

But he couldn't bring himself to do it.

Joseph later wrote, "I had actually seen a light, and in the midst of that light I saw two Personages, and they did in reality speak to me; and though I was hated and persecuted for saying that I had seen a vision, yet it was true; and while they were persecuting me, reviling me, and speaking all manner of evil against me falsely for so saying, I was led to say in my heart: Why persecute me for telling the truth? I have actually seen a vision; and who am I that I can withstand God, or why does the world think to make me deny what I have actually seen? For I had seen a vision; I knew it, and I knew that God knew it, and I could not deny it, neither dared I do it; at least I knew that by so doing I would offend God, and come under condemnation." (JS–H 1:25.)

The Restoration of the True Gospel Unfolds

For more than three years, and without the benefit of further instruction from God, Joseph was tried and tempted for his testimony. Perhaps he was simply being allowed to grow up a little. If he was being tested, he must have passed the test, because on September 21, 1823, the long, laborious process of Restoration began when an angelic visitor named Moroni, a resurrected prophet who had lived anciently on the American continent, appeared to Joseph to tell him that God had a work for him to do. According to Moroni, that work would include: the restoration of the fulness of the true gospel of Jesus Christ; the translation from ancient records of a new book of scripture (now called the Book of Mormon: Another Testament of Jesus Christ); the restoration of priesthood authority (or authority to act in God's name); the fulfillment of Malachi's biblical prophecy about the return of "Elijah the prophet before the coming of the great and dreadful day of the Lord" for the purpose of turning "the heart of the fathers to the children, and the heart of the children to their fathers" (see Malachi 4:5–6); the fulfillment of other biblical prophecies relative to gospel restoration; and preparation for the Second Coming of Christ.

Of course, it didn't all happen at once. Joseph Smith was given time to grow into his assignment. After all, it isn't every day that a backwoods farm boy is called by God to be His designated representative on earth, a living, modern-day prophet. Still, Joseph was remarkably young throughout the entire process. Angelic visitors tutored him until he was ready to begin translating the Book of Mormon in 1827, and they continued to instruct, advise, and counsel him from time to time while he translated. In 1829 God's priesthood authority was restored and the translation of the Book of Mormon was completed. (We'll cover in greater detail the Book of Mormon and the restoration of the priesthood in the next two chapters.)

Through it all, word of the young prophet and his miraculous claims began to spread. As you might expect, the news elicited a wide variety of responses. Some who heard believed, supported, and followed, while others reviled and persecuted. The Smith family suffered ongoing hardships and at the same time received marvelous blessings as a result of Joseph's work. Joseph himself explored the entire range of the human emotional spectrum, from the devastating loss of his beloved brother Alvin in 1823 to his joyful marriage to Emma Hale in 1827.

His spiritual journey was just as diverse. He endured the bitter sorrow of divine rebukes, and he was overwhelmed by magnificent outpourings of heavenly love. Just as He had done with David, Samuel, and Joseph of the Old Testament, God took an innocent, unlearned boy, one still unsullied by the world and pliable to His divine will, and molded and shaped him into His chosen prophet.

The Church of Jesus Christ of Latter-day Saints Officially Organized

On April 6, 1830, some ten years after God had personally responded to a humble, seeking teenager's prayer, The Church of Jesus Christ of Latter-day Saints was officially organized. The time was right. The world was ready. The Great Apostasy was over. God's authority to baptize was restored, and The Church of Jesus Christ was once again fully upon the earth.

Before we can understand the remarkable events that culminated with the organization of the Church in 1830, we should first review the crucial contribution that the Book of Mormon made to the Restoration.

The Book of Mormon

When fourteen-year-old Joseph Smith emerged from the woods that spring morning in 1820 he brought with him new understanding that, as his Grandfather Asael had prophesied, would revolutionize religious thought. He knew for sure that God, our Heavenly Father, and His Son, Jesus Christ, were real, and that they were both exalted, glorified beings. He knew they were two separate, distinct individuals, not just different manifestations of the same eternal God. And he knew that there wasn't a church on the face of the earth Heavenly Father and Jesus felt they could endorse, let alone embrace.

The Heavens Are Not Sealed

But perhaps the most important thing that young Joseph learned that day in what is now referred to by Church members as the Sacred Grove is this significant eternal truth: the heavens are *not* sealed. God is *not* limited. Certainly He isn't bound by the limitations with which some churches try to restrict Him. To those who say that all revelation ended with the death of Christ's original apostles and that we already have all of the instruction from God we will ever need, Joseph Smith's story stands as solemn testimony that God hasn't shut the door on His children. He loves us today just as much as He loved those who lived anciently, and He is just as concerned about us as He was about them. What comfort that sweet assurance provides in a world filled with confusion and discouragement! What peace and security comes to the heart that understands there is a God in heaven who is our Father, who knows us and cares about us—individually and collectively—and who will communicate with us, either directly or through His living prophets, according to our needs.

Admittedly, individuals have enjoyed spiritual guidance and promptings for their personal affairs through the ages. But revelation to prophets had ceased for a time. And the Church organized by the Savior had disappeared from the earth.

As Joseph shared his experience with his family and a few others, there were many who knew he spoke the truth. They felt that comfort and peace. As we have already observed, his family never doubted the veracity of his story, and there were others who were touched by his innocence and sincerity. But there were also those who were outraged by his claims, and they ridiculed and persecuted him for having the audacity to profess divine communion. For the most part, however, life continued as usual for Joseph and the rest of the Smith family for several years after the manifestation that has since come to be known by Latter-day Saints as the First Vision.

But that all changed in the fall of 1823.

Another Divine Visitor

Try to put yourself in the position of the teenage Joseph Smith. You probably don't really understand the ramifications of the experience you've had. But you know that you had it, and you can't help but think that there are certain expectations of you as a result. You continue to pray and to do the things you think you should do, but for several years there have been no answers—at least, nothing as powerful as what you experienced in the woods just three years earlier at age fourteen. And you wonder why.

Although Joseph was firm in his commitment to the reality of his vision, his own historical account of his experience notes that it troubled him that he "was guilty of levity, and sometimes associated with jovial company . . . not consistent with that character which ought to be maintained by one who was called of God. . . . " He began to wonder if his youthful energy and natural cheerfulness were somehow unrighteous and, therefore, the cause of God's continued silence.

If you felt that way, you might be inclined to go to the Lord again—to feel that overwhelming feeling once more and to be reassured of His love and approval. And that is precisely why Joseph dedicated the evening of September 21, 1823 to, in his words, "prayer and supplication to Almighty God for forgiveness of all my sins and follies, and also for a manifestation to me, that I might know of my state and standing before [God]."

Does it seem a little presumptuous for Joseph to assume that he could receive a manifestation from God simply by asking for it? Perhaps. But that was the nature of young Joseph's faith. "I had full confidence in obtaining a divine manifestation," he wrote, "as I previously had one." (JS–H 1:28–29.)

And indeed, the manifestation came—but not quite in the way he expected. This time he was visited by a resurrected being who identified himself as Moroni. And instead of simply telling him that all was well and that God still loved him, Moroni came to put Joseph to work.

An Ancient Sacred Record Revealed

Moroni told Joseph about a sacred record that had been engraved upon plates (or thin sheets) of gold. The record contained an account of several groups of people who inhabited and built remarkable civilizations upon the American continent many hundreds of years earlier. According to Moroni, they also contained "the fulness of the everlasting Gospel . . . as delivered by the Savior to the ancient inhabitants." (JS–H 1:34.)

In fact, the angel Moroni was one of those "ancient inhabitants." Centuries earlier the plates had been entrusted to him by his father, the last of a long line of prophets and leaders who had maintained the record for more than one thousand years. Through times of difficulty and hardship Moroni kept the plates and the sacred information they contained. Eventually he was inspired to hide them for safekeeping, with the understanding that the day would come when God, in His infinite wisdom, would miraculously bring them forth once more.

And now that glorious day had come. Joseph Smith would be the earthly means through which God's miracle would come to pass—as soon as Joseph was ready.

For several years Moroni visited Joseph annually, spiritually preparing him for the task of translating the record as part of the restoration of the fulness of the gospel of Jesus Christ. Now, you might logically ask what such a record might have to do with the Restoration. Perhaps if you know a little more about the book you'll understand why members of The Church of Jesus Christ of Latter-day Saints value it so dearly. Please remember, however, that what follows is only a brief discussion of what appears in the book. In order to fully appreciate the spirit and content of the Book of Mormon, you'll need to read the book for yourself.

Another Testament of Christ

The Book of Mormon: Another Testament of Jesus Christ takes its name from Moroni's father, whose name was Mormon. He was a great prophet who lived on the American

continent about A.D. 400 and who was largely responsible
for accumulating and abridging the material that is found
within the pages of the book. The Book of Mormon is a volume of holy scripture comparable to the Holy Bible in that
it is a record of God's dealings with several groups of ancient
people who migrated to the American continent from the
Holy Land several hundred years before the birth of Christ.
For the most part it deals with the descendants of Lehi, a
prophet who left Jerusalem about 600 B.C., during the first
year of the reign of Zedekiah, king of Judah, shortly before
the Babylonian destruction of Jerusalem.

The Book of Mormon is an interesting mix of Old and
New Testament styles and forms. Just as the Bible compiles
books of scripture written by spiritual leaders such as Moses,
Isaiah, David, Matthew, Luke, and Paul, the Book of Mormon is a compilation of fifteen books, or scriptural accounts,
written by men with names like Nephi, Alma, Helaman,
Mosiah, and Ether. It includes narrative, faith-promoting
stories and experiences, historical accounts of the rise and
fall of entire civilizations, doctrinal essays, testimonies of
the divine mission of the resurrected Lord Jesus Christ, and
prophecy regarding the days in which we live. The center-
piece of the record is a moving account of the appearance of
the Lord Jesus Christ to a group of His "other sheep" (John
10:16) on the American continent soon after His death and
resurrection in Jerusalem.

Messages from the Book of Mormon

The Book of Mormon is full of fascinating reading. You
won't, for example, find a better adventure story than the
experience of Ammon, who was employed as a servant to a
king and ended up converting the king and his entire house-
hold to Christ and His Church after courageously defending
the royal flocks (see Alma 17–19). Nor will you read a finer
doctrinal treatise on faith than the one in the thirty-second

chapter of Alma. And there just isn't a sweeter story anywhere than the remarkable account of Christ's personal ministry among these people, especially the part where Jesus asks them to bring their children to Him, and He blesses them "one by one" and prays for them (see 3 Nephi 17).

The following brief passages of scripture, taken from several different locations in the Book of Mormon, demonstrate the simple eloquence and power of this book:

"And it came to pass that I, Nephi, said unto my father: I will go and do the things which the Lord hath commanded, for I know that the Lord giveth no commandments unto the children of men, save he shall prepare a way for them that they may accomplish the thing which he commandeth them." (1 Nephi 3:7.)

"And we talk of Christ, we rejoice in Christ, we preach of Christ, we prophesy of Christ, and we write according to our prophecies, that our children may know to what source they may look for a remission of their sins." (2 Nephi 25:26.)

"And behold, I tell you these things that ye may learn wisdom; that ye may learn that when ye are in the service of your fellow beings ye are only in the service of your God." (Mosiah 2:17.)

"Believe in God; believe that he is, and that he created all things, both in heaven and in earth; believe that he has all wisdom, and all power, both in heaven and in earth; believe that man doth not comprehend all the things which the Lord can comprehend. And again, believe that ye must repent of your sins and forsake them, and humble yourselves before God; and ask in sincerity of heart that he would forgive you; and now, if you believe all these things see that ye do them." (Mosiah 4:9–10.)

"O, remember, my son, and learn wisdom in thy youth; yea, learn in thy youth to keep the commandments of God." (Alma 37:35.)

"Now they never had fought, yet they did not fear death;

and they did think more upon the liberty of their fathers than they did upon their lives; yea, they had been taught by their mothers, that if they did not doubt, God would deliver them.

"And they rehearsed unto me the words of their mothers, saying: We do not doubt our mothers knew it." (Alma 56:47–48.)

The Bible and the Book of Mormon

Members of The Church of Jesus Christ of Latter-day Saints not only love the Book of Mormon but believe it to be the word of God. That doesn't take away from their belief in the Holy Bible and its timeless and inspired teachings. Rather, the two books serve as companion volumes of scripture, each one reinforcing the message and doctrine of the other. I should also mention that Latter-day Saints recognize two other volumes of scripture: the Doctrine and Covenants, a compilation of revelations given through Joseph Smith and other presidents of the Church, and the Pearl of Great Price, which contains other prophetic translations and historical records, including Joseph Smith's autobiographical account of his experiences, from which I have quoted within these pages.

That brings us to the second thing you should know about the Book of Mormon. One of the great difficulties many Christians have with the Book of Mormon and other scriptures of The Church of Jesus Christ of Latter-day Saints stems from a sincere belief that the Bible contains all the truth they'll ever need. I understand that concern and share their deep affection for the Bible. But I must tell you in all sincerity that my love for my Savior and my commitment to Christianity have been intensified and strengthened by the Book of Mormon, in part because it helps me understand many of the doctrinal questions the Bible leaves unanswered.

For example, the New Testament makes it abundantly clear that baptism is an essential gospel ordinance. Even Christ was baptized "to fulfil all righteousness." (Matthew 3:15.) But there seems to be some confusion in the Christian world today about who needs to be baptized. Some churches teach that little children are born in sin, and therefore need to be baptized immediately. Others cite Christ's teaching regarding children that "of such is the kingdom of heaven" (Matthew 19:14), and believe that baptism is strictly an adult ordinance.

As inspired—and inspiring—as the Bible is, you won't find a definitive answer to this dilemma there. But you will find one in the Book of Mormon.

"Behold I say unto you that this thing shall ye teach—repentance and baptism unto those who are accountable and capable of committing sin," the prophet Mormon taught his son Moroni. "Yea, teach parents that they must repent and be baptized, and humble themselves as their little children, and they shall all be saved with their little children.

"And their little children need no repentance, neither baptism. Behold, baptism is unto repentance to the fulfilling the commandments unto the remission of sins.

"But little children are alive in Christ, even from the foundation of the world; if not so, God is a partial God, and also a changeable God, and a respecter to persons; for how many little children have died without baptism!" (Moroni 8:10–12.)

The issue is further clarified in a revelation to the Prophet Joseph Smith found in the Doctrine and Covenants, wherein the Lord indicates that children should be baptized at eight years of age. (See D&C 68:27.)

What a blessing it is to have additional understanding about divine doctrine that can increase our knowledge of Heavenly Father and enhance our relationship with Him!

And infant baptism is just one of many issues and doctrines that receive illumination within the pages of the Book

48

of Mormon. Have you ever wondered exactly what it means to be resurrected? While the subject is mentioned in the Bible, there isn't much elaboration. But a Book of Mormon prophet named Amulek explained it this way:

"The spirit and the body shall be reunited again in its perfect form; both limb and joint shall be restored to its proper frame, even as we now are at this time; and we shall be brought to stand before God, knowing even as we know now, and have a bright recollection of all our guilt.

"Now, this restoration shall come to all," Amulek continued, "both old and young, both bond and free, both male and female, both the wicked and the righteous; and even there shall not so much as a hair of their heads be lost; but every thing shall be restored to its perfect frame. . . . " (Alma 11:43–44.)

Similar enlightenment can be found with regard to the fall of Adam (see 2 Nephi 2), the atonement of Christ (see Alma 42), and even the Book of Mormon itself, including an explanation of how you can know for yourself whether or not the book is the word of God (see Moroni 10:3–5). The Book of Mormon offers pure, concise doctrine that hasn't been tampered with by religious philosophers, councils, panels, and kings. Unlike the evolutionary process that has given us our Bible, the Book of Mormon underwent only one translation between its original imprinting on plates of gold and its appearance in 1830 as the paper-and-ink manifestation of the restored gospel of Jesus Christ.

Testimonies of the Book of Mormon

And that's the final thing we need to talk about relative to the Book of Mormon. Although more than seven years had passed between the First Vision and the time Joseph Smith finally was entrusted with the gold plates and allowed to begin the work of translation, very little actually changed in terms of his physical preparation for the task. He was still a poor, relatively uneducated, and backwoodsy young man from upstate New York. While he had been taught by angels, most of that instruction was aimed at building his gospel knowledge and faith and strengthening his spiritual sensitivity. The actual translation of the plates, a laborious process of dictation and hand-written copy, was not the result of newly acquired knowledge and skills. It was a miracle—nothing more, nothing less. God took a simple, faithful young man by the hand, and together they changed the face of contemporary religion.

More than thirty years after Joseph's death, his wife, Emma, was interviewed by her son, Joseph Smith III. She was no longer closely associated with the Church, and she had long since remarried. Still, as one of only a few first-hand witnesses to the translation of the Book of Mormon, her testimony is compelling.

"Joseph Smith could neither write nor dictate a coherent and well-worded letter, let alone dictate a book like the Book of Mormon," Emma told her son, "and though I was an active participant during the translation of the plates, and had cognizance of things as they transpired, it is marvelous to me—a marvel and a wonder—as much as to anyone else.

"My belief is that the Book of Mormon is of divine authenticity—I have not the slightest doubt of it," she continued. "I am satisfied that no man could have dictated the writing of the manuscripts unless he was inspired; for, when acting as his scribe, your father would dictate to me hour after hour; and when returning after meals, or interruptions, he would at once begin where he had left off, without either seeing the manuscript or having any portion of it read to him. This was a usual thing for him to do. It would have been improbable that a learned man could do this, and for one so ignorant and unlearned as he was, it was simply impossible." (Joseph Smith Letter Books, Historical Department, The Church of Jesus Christ of Latter-day Saints, page 1.)

Similar testimonies were offered by others who worked closely with the prophet during the translation process. Near the front of each copy of the Book of Mormon are two such testimonies, one signed by three men and another signed by eight men, each of whom claims to have been a witness to the divinity of the book. Included among these witnesses are several who eventually left the Church. But even though they may have had difficulty with persecution or even differences with Joseph Smith or later Church leaders, none ever denied his testimony that the Book of Mormon came forth through the gift and power of God.

You Can Know the Truth of the Book of Mormon

As significant as those testimonies are, however, the most important witness of the veracity of the Book of Mormon is the witness of the Holy Spirit to individual believers. Near the end of the Book of Mormon, Moroni makes this meaningful promise: "And when ye shall receive these things, I would exhort you that ye would ask God, the Eternal Father, in the name of Christ, if these things are not true; and if ye shall ask with a sincere heart, with real intent, having faith in Christ, he will manifest the truth of it unto you, by the power of the Holy Ghost. And by the power of the Holy Ghost ye may know the truth of all things." (Moroni 10:4–5.)

It is by that power that I have gained a deep and abiding testimony of the Book of Mormon. I know the Book of Mormon is the word of God because I have read it many, many times. I have pondered over it. I have prayed and asked God to tell me if it is true. I have received the witness of truth as it comes to a man or a woman—the only way it *can* come—through the power of the Holy Ghost, which gives me the peaceful assurance that the Book of Mormon is true. As a result of studying and living by the teachings of the Book of Mormon, I have come to know the Lord better, and I have used His teachings from the Book of Mormon to strengthen my children and grandchildren.

The Apostle Paul encouraged the Thessalonian saints: "Prove all things; hold fast that which is good." (1 Thessalonians 5:21.) It is my simple, sincere belief that anyone who will take the time to prove the Book of Mormon—that is, study it, ponder about it, and ask God to tell you if it is true—will want to "hold fast" to it because it is, indeed, the word of God. As the second great Book of Mormon prophet, Nephi, said: "And if ye shall believe in Christ ye will believe in these words, for they are the words of Christ, and he hath given them unto me; and they teach all men that they should do good." (2 Nephi 33:10.)

Nephi's message is the central focus of the Book of Mormon: bringing people to Christ and teaching them "that they should do good." And according to the prophet Mormon, that's an excellent indication that the book is worthy of your time and consideration. He wrote:

"For every thing which inviteth to do good, and to persuade to believe in Christ, is sent forth by the power and gift of Christ; wherefore ye may know with a perfect knowledge it is of God.

"But whatsoever thing persuadeth men to do evil, and believe not in Christ, and deny him, and serve not God, then ye may know with a perfect knowledge it is of the devil; for after this manner doth the devil work, for he persuadeth no man to do good, no, not one; neither do his angels; neither do they who subject themselves unto him.

"Wherefore, I beseech of you, brethren, that ye should search diligently in the light of Christ that ye may know good from evil; and if ye will lay hold upon every good thing, and condemn it not, ye certainly will be a child of Christ." (Moroni 7:16–17, 19.)

That's wise scriptural counsel—for yesterday, today, and forever.

The Priesthood of God

Let's imagine for a moment that you and I are both driving down the freeway in our cars—me behind you—when you forget to signal before changing lanes.

Immediately I start honking my horn and flashing my lights. I pull up alongside your car and signal for you to pull over. We both move to the side of the road and stop. I get out of my car, march up to your window, and inform you that you have committed a traffic violation and that I intend to enforce the law.

What are you going to do?

You're probably going to ask to see my law enforcement credentials, aren't you? You're going to want to know what right I have to enforce the laws of the land—the possibility of a citizen's arrest notwithstanding. You're going to question my authority. You will not accept my actions to enforce the traffic laws without a clear identification of my authority.

Authority is one of those concepts that most people seem to inherently understand—probably because it governs almost every facet of our lives, and has done so for as long as most of us can remember. When we were in school we automatically acknowledged that teachers and administrators had the authority to tell us what to do. Today, when the

53

boss tells us to do something, we do it. When a law is passed, we obey it. When we hear that police siren behind us, we pull over. And when I'm in your home—or your car or your business—you're in charge, and it wouldn't be right for me to tell you what to do or to make decisions in your behalf without your approval or permission.

That's just the way it is in this world. And I'm grateful, as I'm sure you are, for this reality. Although the concept of authority places some inherent limits on our absolute freedom, without it we would have anarchy, complete chaos. Can you imagine a world where anyone could do anything at any time—with or without permission? There is safety in authority, including the spiritual safety of God's authority.

Priesthood Authority Can Only Come from God

Joseph Smith longed for that spiritual safety. As we have already mentioned, he lived in a time and place of considerable religious feeling. In his search for truth he came in contact with many different ministers, each one claiming authority from God. His desire to be baptized into Heavenly Father's true church motivated his earnest prayer to God in the Sacred Grove. But even though Joseph learned through that experience that none of the existing churches' claims were true, it wasn't until he was well into the work of translating the Book of Mormon that the need for real priesthood authority from God became clear to him.

According to Joseph, it was the book's teachings concerning baptism that caused him to wonder about this doctrinal concept. The more he and Oliver Cowdery, who was assisting as his scribe at this point, translated, the more they learned about the importance of "following your Lord and your Savior down into the water, according to his word." (2 Nephi 31:13.) They were humbled by the prophet Nephi's reasoning that "if the Lamb of God, he being holy, should have need to be baptized by water, to fulfil all righteous-

54

ness, O then, how much more need have we, being unholy, to be baptized, yea, even by water!" (2 Nephi 31:5.) And they were thrilled by the Lord's promise that "he that is baptized in my name, to him will the Father give the Holy Ghost, like unto me; wherefore, follow me, and do the things which ye have seen me do." (2 Nephi 31:12.)

But that created a problem. While it was clear that baptism was essential in God's kingdom, it was equally clear that not just anyone was authorized to perform the ordinance. Joseph and Oliver had read that Alma baptized his people "having authority from the Almighty God." (Mosiah 18:13.) And they were familiar with Paul's ministerial declaration to the Hebrews that "no man taketh this honour unto himself, but he that is called of God, as was Aaron." (Hebrews 5:4.) They were probably also familiar with the Old Testament explanation that Aaron was called to his priesthood position by his brother, the prophet Moses, who held God's authority (see Exodus 28:1), and that it was common in those days for someone who was called to a holy calling to receive authority through the laying on of hands— once again by those authorized to do so (see Numbers 27:18).

Based on what he had learned from many heavenly sources during the previous several years, Joseph Smith knew that God's full priesthood authority was no longer on the earth. So how could he and others partake of the blessings of baptism? Joseph understood that he didn't have the right to "take this honor unto himself." But where was God's authorized representative who could provide the blessing?

The Aaronic Priesthood Is Restored

Joseph and Oliver anguished over the dilemma. Finally they decided to take the problem to the Lord. On May 15, 1829, they found an isolated spot on the banks of the Susquehanna River near Harmony, Pennsylvania, and humbly poured out the desires of their hearts to God. While they were praying they were visited by a heavenly messenger: John the Baptist, now resurrected. This was the same John who, by virtue of the authority he held, had baptized Jesus Christ in the Jordan River nearly two thousand years earlier.

John the Baptist told Joseph Smith and Oliver Cowdery that God had sent him to restore priesthood authority to the earth, which had been lost since the dissolution of the Council of Twelve Apostles shortly after A.D. 100. He placed his hands upon their heads and pronounced these powerful words: "Upon you my fellow servants, in the name of Messiah I confer the Priesthood of Aaron, which holds the keys of the ministering of angels, and of the gospel of repentance, and of baptism by immersion for the remission of sins; and this shall never be taken again from the earth, until the sons of Levi do offer again an offering unto the Lord in righteousness." (D&C 13.)

John the Baptist told Joseph and Oliver that "this Aaronic Priesthood had not the power of laying on hands for the gift of the Holy Ghost, but that this should be conferred on us hereafter," Joseph Smith wrote in his history, which is recorded in the book of scripture called the Pearl of Great Price. "And he commanded us to go and be baptized, and gave us directions that I should baptize Oliver Cowdery, and that afterwards he should baptize me.

"Accordingly we went and were baptized. I baptized him first, and afterwards he baptized me—after which I laid my hands upon his head and ordained him to the Aaronic Priesthood, and afterwards he laid his hands on me and ordained me to the same Priesthood—for so we were commanded." (JS–H 1:70–71.)

As you might expect, baptism by complete immersion in the waters of the Susquehanna River (which was according to the instructions they were given) and ordination to the priesthood was an incredible experience for both men. Joseph recorded that they "experienced great and glorious blessings from our Heavenly Father" immediately after coming out of the waters of baptism.

"We were filled with the Holy Ghost," he said, "and rejoiced in the God of our Salvation." (JS–H 1:73.)

The Melchizedek Priesthood Is Restored

As John the Baptist indicated, Joseph and Oliver received the Priesthood of Aaron, or the Aaronic Priesthood, and they were thrilled with the blessing and opportunity it brought into their lives. But as they continued their work they began to understand what their heavenly visitor had said about limitations to Aaronic Priesthood authority. They could baptize, but they did not have the authority to perform many of the priesthood functions that Christ and His Apostles performed, such as conferring the gift of the Holy Ghost and administering to heal the sick. And Joseph was quite sure he didn't have the authority he would need to reorganize Christ's Church on the earth, even though he knew he was being prepared for that task. So just a short time after they received the Aaronic Priesthood, Joseph and Oliver again sought the privacy of the wilderness to petition the Lord for understanding.

And once again, the Lord responded miraculously. This time Joseph and Oliver were visited by Peter, James, and John, three of the original Twelve Apostles that Jesus Himself had ordained with priesthood authority. Peter, James, and John placed their hands on Joseph and Oliver's heads and conferred the Melchizedek Priesthood, a greater, more comprehensive form of priesthood authority. This priesthood takes its name from Melchizedek, one of the great high priests of Old Testament times. It includes God's authority to perform *all* of the ordinances of the gospel of Jesus Christ. It also gave Joseph all of the priesthood authority he would need to restore the fulness of the gospel of Jesus Christ on the earth. Thus Joseph Smith was authorized by God to organize His Church, The Church of Jesus Christ of Latter-day Saints.

Priesthood authority was essential for Joseph Smith and the significant mission he had to perform, just as it has always been an indispensable part of Heavenly Father's complete ministry among His children on earth. Through priesthood authority we have access to essential gospel ordinances such as baptism. Just as the Syrian captain Naaman was cured of his leprosy by following the instructions of the prophet Elisha to wash himself seven times in the Jordan River (2 Kings 5:1–14), so too are we blessed as we perform the outward ordinances of the gospel under the direction of those to whom God has given His authority.

"Ye Have Not Chosen Me"

Historically, the Lord has been selective about those to whom He gives His authority. "Ye have not chosen me," Jesus reminded His Apostles, "but I have chosen you, and ordained you." (John 15:16.) The priesthood is the power and authority of God given to worthy men to perform all of the ordinances of salvation that are necessary for men *and* women to gain all of the promised blessings of God, including eternal exaltation in His presence. It is the power through which the world was created, and miracles have been wrought from the time of Adam until the present day. According to John Taylor, the third president of The Church of Jesus Christ of Latter-day Saints, priesthood "is the government of God, whether on the earth or in the heavens, for it is by that power, agency or principle that all things are governed on the earth and in the heavens, and by that power that all things are upheld and sustained. It governs all things, it directs all things, it sustains all things, and has to do with all things that God and truth are associated with."

(*The Millennial Star,* November 1, 1847, 9:321.) Although the Lord has chosen to bestow priesthood authority upon men, it should be noted that priesthood isn't about gender as much as it is about responsibility.

Today in Latter-day Saint congregations around the world, young men ordained to the Aaronic Priesthood officiate in the preparation, blessing, and distribution of the sacramental emblems of Christ's flesh and blood during weekly worship services. They are also authorized to perform baptisms, gather donations to help the poor, and minister to members of the Church in their homes. Meanwhile, those who are ordained to the Melchizedek Priesthood conduct church services, perform sacred ordinances, and give blessings of physical, spiritual, and emotional healing. Through the priesthood Latter-day Saints may draw upon the powers of heaven as a way of blessing their own lives as well as the lives of others.

Inasmuch as I've been speaking about the need for God's authority among those who claim to represent Him, you would be justified in posing the same question to me that I posed to that gathering of ministers my missionaries in Canada arranged for me to address: Where does *my* authority come from? And I'm pleased to be able to respond.

Where Does My Authority Come From?

I was ordained an Apostle (an office in the Melchizedek Priesthood) on October 10, 1985, by Gordon B. Hinckley, who was ordained by David O. McKay, who was ordained by Joseph F. Smith, who was ordained by Brigham Young (yes, *that* Brigham Young), who received his ordination from the Three Witnesses to the Book of Mormon (which included Oliver Cowdery, Martin Harris, and David Whitmer, whose collective testimony is among those found near the front of each copy of the Book of Mormon), who were ordained by Joseph Smith and Oliver Cowdery, who were ordained by

Peter, James, and John, who were ordained under the hands of Jesus Christ.

In other words, in just eight steps I can trace my apostolic priesthood authority back to the ultimate source of all priesthood authority in The Church of Jesus Christ of Latter-day Saints: the Lord Jesus Christ Himself.

Please understand that I don't say this to boast. I am very grateful to the Lord for the privilege of serving Him. I recognize and freely acknowledge that my authority to act in God's name isn't really mine; it is His. But it would be wrong if I didn't also tell you that I have complete and total confidence in the power of the priesthood of God given to me through His duly ordained representatives.

It should be noted, however, that the mere fact that a man holds the priesthood isn't enough in and of itself to give him any kind of authority. Those who are ordained to the priesthood must diligently strive to keep God's commandments. The Lord taught Joseph Smith that "no power or influence can or ought to be maintained by virtue of the priesthood." Rather, the Lord said, that influence comes as a result of living such Christian virtues as persuasion, long-suffering, gentleness and meekness, love unfeigned, and kindness and pure knowledge, "which shall greatly enlarge the soul without hypocrisy and without guile." (D&C 121:41–42.)

The Lord also warned Joseph that "when we undertake to cover our sins, or to gratify our pride, our vain ambition, or to exercise control or dominion or compulsion upon the souls of the children of men, in any degree of unrighteousness, behold, the heavens withdraw themselves; the Spirit of the Lord is grieved; and when it is withdrawn, Amen to the priesthood or the authority of that man." (D&C 121:37.)

In other words, one who is not striving to be obedient to God's commandments is not worthy to represent Him here upon the earth. Of course, that doesn't mean all priesthood

60

bearers are expected to live perfect lives—Christ alone was capable of such perfection. But they are expected to do the very best they can to live righteously and worthy of the power they possess.

Priesthood Provides the Power to Do Good

When faith and faithfulness are added to priesthood authority, marvelous things can happen in the lives of men, women, and families. We learn in the scriptures that after the Lord "called unto him his twelve disciples, he gave them power against unclean spirits, to cast them out, and to heal all manner of sickness and all manner of disease." (Matthew 10:1; see also Mark 3:14; Mark 6:7; and Luke 9:1.) It was that same priesthood authority that Peter employed when he healed the lame beggar outside the temple in Jerusalem soon after the day of Pentecost.

"Silver and gold have I none," Peter said to the beggar, "but such as I have give I thee: In the name of Jesus Christ of Nazareth rise up and walk.

"And he took him by the right hand, and lifted him up: and immediately his feet and ankle bones received strength.

"And he leaping up stood, and walked, and entered with them into the temple, walking and leaping, and praising God." (Acts 3:6–8.)

Such great and powerful miracles of healing, restoration, and revelation righteously enacted through the authority of the priesthood occur in our day as well. May I share one experience of my own?

Some years ago I heard a young woman talk about the physical struggle her older sister was having with her health during a difficult pregnancy. I was touched by the story and concerned about the girl's sister and her unborn child, and I wished there was something I could do for her. But it wasn't until later that evening while I was reading the scriptures that the unmistakable impression came that I needed to visit this sick member of the Church. Having received similar promptings from time to time, I have learned not to question them but to simply respond. So I asked my wife to go with me to visit this young wife and mother.

"I don't know for sure why I'm here," I said when her husband answered our knock at their door, "except that I have had a strong prompting that I need to see your wife."

"Brother Ballard," the young husband replied, "I don't think she'll see you. She has been so sick she hasn't seen anyone."

"Please just tell her that we're here," I said, "and *why* we're here."

While waiting we browsed through some of the family photographs on display in the living room. There was a picture of one of their children, who was seriously disabled. There was also a photograph of a younger child, healthy in every way and anxious to have a new little brother or sister with whom to play. My wife reminded me of the stillborn child that had been born to the couple, as well as the unusual physical toll each pregnancy had taken on this young mother. The decision to have another child must have been difficult for the couple. They had likely made the matter a subject of the most careful, prayerful consideration, and had received spiritual assurance that all would be well—which doubtless made the current crisis all the more disconcerting.

At last the woman joined us in the living room. She was obviously weak and in considerable pain, suffering with a severe case of shingles that covered the left side of her face and neck with huge, blistered lesions. According to the husband, her blood platelet level was so low that her life—as well as the life of her baby—was at risk.

I took her hand in mine and told her the simple truth: "The Lord has sent me here to give you a blessing." Her husband, his father, and I placed our hands on her head, and I felt spiritually impressed to give her a blessing of complete and total healing.

"At that moment," she later wrote of the experience, "I felt a force move through my body and out through my toes. . . . I know the Spirit of the Lord was there, Brother Ballard. I felt it. I heard it speak through you. . . . It gave me the strength to faithfully endure and accomplish a task that seemed impossible. After the blessing I knew in my heart that we would be blessed with a healthy baby.

And they were.

"Our new little son has been such a light and great joy in our life," the young mother wrote. "Through this little guy the Lord sent us a beautiful gift of love."

There Is Power in Priesthood Ordinances

Wondrous miracles do happen through the authority of the priesthood. In most instances, however, priesthood authority works quietly and simply in the lives of those who respect and live worthy of it. It enables believers to make sacred covenants with the Lord through baptism, and to renew those covenants each week at Church services through partaking of the sacrament of the Lord's Supper. Priesthood blessings offer comfort and peace and the courage to cope with life's challenges. And priesthood offices authorize Church leaders to officiate in the administration of the Church in their respective callings and assignments.

Nowhere is the beauty and power of priesthood authority more clearly seen than in the sacred, holy buildings we call temples. Perhaps you've seen one of our temples, or even visited one. Temples are different from our meetinghouses, where regular Sunday services and weekday activities are held. Temples are a place apart, where worthy, faithful, devoted members go to perform sacred religious ordinances not just for time, but for all eternity.

Now, I recognize how presumptuous that may sound: a

63

man claiming authority that extends into the heavens. But please remember that it is God's authority, and it is only limited to the extent that He wishes it to be limited. And remember the words of the Lord to those to whom He had given His authority anciently: "Whatsoever ye shall bind on earth shall be bound in heaven: and whatsoever ye shall loose on earth shall be loosed in heaven." (Matthew 18:18.) Clearly there is divine precedent for our belief that priesthood authority is eternal.

Of all the opportunities my priesthood authority affords, there is none grander than the privilege of being in one of our temples and representing the Master in officiating in the marriage of two of His worthy, righteous children. No matter who they are or where they come from, they always look resplendent, with the glow of love and faith shining in their eyes. Usually there are other family members and friends present to make it a sweet, intimate occasion.

It should be noted that temple weddings are a little different from other weddings. Because they're held in the temple, only faithful members of the Church can attend. Nor is there any of the pomp and ceremony one normally associates with big church weddings—no music, no processional, no chapel trimmed with ribbons and flowers. Please don't misunderstand—a temple wedding is a supremely beautiful and joyful occasion, just as it should be. But it is also simple, profound, and eloquently reverent.

The most unusual thing about temple weddings, however, has to do with the words that are used by the one who officiates at the ceremony. Most weddings outside the temple include language that limits the term of the marriage— an automatic bill of divorcement, if you will. The presiding authority will usually unite the happy couple "until death do you part," or words to that effect. But in a temple marriage the newlyweds understand that their marriage, performed by one holding the priesthood, will last forever—

throughout time *and* eternity—and the words of the ceremony reflect that glorious concept. The couple isn't just married; they are "sealed" to each other through God's authority for "time and for all eternity." According to Latter-day Saint doctrine, that couple will be together forever, as long as the man and woman are faithful to each other and to Heavenly Father's commandments.

We believe that marriage is ordained of God. The Doctrine and Covenants explains, "Whoso forbiddeth to marry is not ordained of God, for marriage is ordained of God unto man." (D&C 49:15.)

"The marriage sanctioned by God provides men and women with the opportunity to fulfill their divine potentials. 'Neither is the man without the woman, neither the woman without the man, in the Lord' (1 Cor. 11:11). Husbands and wives are unique in some ways and free to develop their eternal gifts, yet as coequals in the sight of their heavenly parents they are one in the divine goals they pursue, in their devotion to eternal principles and ordinances, in their obedience to the Lord, and in their divine love for each other. When a man and woman who have been sealed together in a temple are united spiritually, mentally, emotionally, and physically, taking full responsibility for nurturing each other, they are truly married. Together they strive to emulate the prototype of the heavenly home from which they came. The Church teaches them to complement, support, and enrich one another. . . . If a husband and wife are faithful to their temple marriage, they will continue as co-creators in God's celestial kingdom through the eternities." (*Encyclopedia of Mormonism*, 4 vols., Daniel H. Ludlow, ed. [New York: Macmillan, 1992], 2:487.)

The principle of eternal marriage is a doctrine unique to The Church of Jesus Christ of Latter-day Saints. Couples who marry in the temple and who make covenants that enable them to become an eternal family unit feel a great sense of purpose and destiny about their relationship with each other as well as with the children they bring into the world. The importance of raising children and creating strong families seems all the more vital to those who believe they can live together forever.

What a glorious, reassuring knowledge! Doesn't it make sense that our Heavenly Father, who loves us and wants us to progress, would provide a way for men and women who are devoted to each other's eternal happiness to take their relationship into the next life? As President Brigham Young said, eternal marriage "is the thread which runs from the beginning to the end of the holy Gospel of Salvation—of the Gospel of the Son of God; it is from eternity to eternity." (*Discourses of Brigham Young,* John A. Widtsoe, ed. [Salt Lake City: Deseret Book, 1971], p. 195.)

Families Can Be Forever

On numerous occasions I visit with religious leaders from other faiths. Frequently they express interest in the emphasis we place on marriage and the family. I recall one instance when this subject came up in a conversation with ministers from another denomination. These religious leaders complimented the Church by saying they knew of no other organization that had done as much to preserve and build families. I thanked them for their kindness, and then they expressed concern about the number of people in their own congregations who were succumbing to the temptations of the world, adding that they believed the only cure to be in building stronger homes. When they asked if we'd share some of our family-related materials with them, we were happy to do so.

After we had talked for some time about things we do to strengthen families, I felt a need to be honest with these men about one issue we hadn't addressed. "I hope I won't offend you by what I'm going to say," I began. "You're welcome to anything we have on helping families, and you may implement any of our ideas and programs. But I don't think our materials will work for you the same way they work for us."

When they asked why, I answered, "There is a fundamental difference in the way we view the family. When a husband and wife marry in the temple, and later welcome children into their home, they look at the entire experience of child-rearing and family-building with an eternal perspective. Even though our families face normal challenges and problems, they try to see past the here-and-now and make decisions that will keep their family strong and cohesive because they truly believe they can be together forever."

That perspective makes all the difference, and it begins when a man and woman kneel at an altar in one of our dedicated temples.

I'll never forget performing the temple marriage for my son and his wonderful bride. It was one of the first temple marriages I ever performed, and to tell the truth, I think I was just as nervous about it as they were—though I wasn't exactly sure why. As a bishop in the Church I had performed a number of marriages outside of the temple for those who chose not to be married in the temple, or who were not eligible to go there, but who wanted their ceremony performed by a Latter-day Saint bishop nonetheless. But none of those marriages was eternal. This was going to be different. This was forever. And if I was going to do something that would last forever, I wanted to be absolutely sure that I did it right.

I needn't have worried. Once we all settled into our places in one of the beautiful temple sealing rooms, we were engulfed by that extraordinary feeling of love and peace that exists in such rich abundance in the sacred building we respectfully call "The House of the Lord." I looked at my son and his lovely wife-to-be as they knelt across from each other at the temple altar and I realized two things. First, I could see in their eyes their commitment to one another that brought them to this precious moment. And second, I realized that these wonderful young people were ready and worthy to begin a glorious eternal adventure together. Of course, they didn't have a full understanding of what that really meant right then. But because of Heavenly Father's priesthood authority, they would have all eternity to live and love and learn and grow.

Together.

Was I able to perform that marvelous eternal ordinance just because I wanted to, or because my son asked me to do it? Could I do it simply because it seemed like the right thing to do? No. I could only do it because I had been ordained and given authority from God to do so. Without that authority I could do nothing. If I didn't hold the Lord's authority I wouldn't presume to teach the gospel, baptize, preside at meetings, or give blessings. And I certainly wouldn't claim the authority to perform marriages that would bind people to each other through the eternities without authorization from the God of eternities.

That would be like pulling someone over on the freeway to enforce traffic regulations without a badge of authority. And we both know I'd never do anything like that.

God's
Eternal Plan

Of all the experiences this life has to offer, few are as compelling and powerful as mortality's bookends: birth and death. One cannot look into the face of an infant, minutes old, and not wonder: "Where did you come from, little one? Did you just *happen,* or are you part of something larger—something grand and eternal? What do you know? What could you tell me if only you had the capacity? And what promise does life have in store for you?"

I know. I've asked myself those questions at least seven times—once for each of our seven children.

Similarly profound questions often accompany the death of a loved one. Is the end of mortality the end of life? Is there something else out there to give additional meaning and purpose to our existence? If so, what does that mean to us—here and now? Does the way we choose to live our lives really matter? And what will be the nature of our most cherished relationships in the life after life?

For members of The Church of Jesus Christ of Latter-day Saints, those questions have answers that are filled with comfort, peace, and the love of God. Through latter-day scriptures such as the Book of Mormon and continuous revelation to living prophets and apostles, we have learned that our lives here on earth have meaning because they are part of our Heavenly Father's glorious plan for our eternal happiness.

We Lived as Spirit Children of Our Heavenly Father

This plan originated long before any of us were born. Before the world was created, we all lived as the spirit children of our Heavenly Father. Through a natural process of inheritance we received in embryo the traits and attributes of our Heavenly Father. We are His spirit children. Some of what our Eternal Father is, we have inherited. What he has become *we* may become. (For scriptural enlightenment on this important concept, please see Acts 17:29 and Romans 8:16.)

Life in our heavenly home was a little different from life on earth, as we weren't subject to the frailties and challenges of mortality. But we were still very much involved with learning and growing, maturing and developing; and we had meaningful association with one another. We had the opportunity in our premortal existence to make decisions and choices, and some of us proved to be better at that than others.

"Families on earth are an extension of the family of God. According to the LDS concept of the family, every person is a child of heavenly parents as well as mortal parents. Each individual was created spiritually and physically in the image of God and Christ (Moses 2:27; 3:5). The First Presidency has declared, 'All men and women are in the similitude of the universal Father and Mother, and are literally the sons and daughters of Deity' (*Messages of the First Presidency*, 4:203). Everyone, before coming to this earth, lived with Heavenly Father and Heavenly Mother, and each was loved and taught by them as a member of their eternal family." (*Encyclopedia of Mormonism*, 2:486–87.)

Our Heavenly Parents' love and concern for us continues to this very moment. In our wonderful, pre-earth home we had the opportunity to learn many eternal truths. Our Heavenly Father wanted us to develop every godly quality, for He knew that although each of us is unique, we all have within us the seeds of godhood. Indeed, we yearned to be like Him. But He understood that we could only progress to a certain point without the wisdom of experience through mortality, including the trials and temptations that come to all of us as a direct result of our physical bodies. Therefore our Father's plan was created to help us reach our full potential. It would be difficult and sometimes painful—for Him, perhaps, as well as for us. But He knew it was the only way His children could grow and improve.

We Chose God's Plan before We Were Born

So our Father called all of His spirit children together to explain His plan. He told us that He had created a world for us where we could gain experience and be tested in a wide variety of ways. Part of that test included complete forgetfulness of our heavenly home. This would be necessary so that we could make real choices between right and wrong without being swayed by our memories of what it was like to live with God. As Paul explained to the Corinthians, we were to "walk by faith, not by sight." (2 Corinthians 5:7.)

But He promised not to leave us entirely alone. The Holy Ghost, he said, would help us make good choices if we listened to its gentle promptings. He would also reveal His will to prophets and inspire the creation of scriptures to guide and direct us.

Even with all of that, however, Heavenly Father knew we would fall short of perfection from time to time. So He promised that a Savior would be provided to atone for our bad decisions and choices and make it possible for all of us to eventually become clean and pure enough to return to live with Him.

But the choice would always be ours. As much as He wanted us to return to live with Him, He could not and would not force His will upon us. The plan had at its very foundation the principle of moral agency, which could be exercised for good or ill. That meant God was leaving it up to us to determine whether or not we would return to His eternal home through His Son, Jesus Christ.

Unfortunately, some of our spirit brothers and sisters didn't like God's plan. One of them, Lucifer, was especially displeased, and he rebelled against it. He proposed that the plan be altered so that obedience to God would not be optional, nor would there be any right for us to choose. All mortals would be forced to do good, which meant that none would be lost. But there was a catch to Lucifer's deceitful suggestion: in return for his impossible promise to save all of humanity, he demanded that all of the honor and glory go to him—not the Father.

Jesus, God's firstborn and the wisest and greatest of Heavenly Father's spirit children, knew that only the Father could be so honored. He volunteered to assume the most critical role in His Father's plan, with all of the glory going to God. Jesus said He would come to earth to provide the example of a perfect life, and then He would willingly suffer the burden and pains of our sins so that the rest of us could return to our Heavenly Home—if we *choose* to do so. According to Heavenly Father's plan, it was absolutely critical that each individual be free to choose.

In fact, that freedom even extended into our premortal existence. All of Heavenly Father's spirit children had the privilege of choosing between the two plans presented. Unhappily, one-third of the host of heaven chose to follow Lucifer (see D&C 29:36). In so doing, they chose to deny themselves the benefits and blessings of mortality, which means they ultimately expelled themselves from God's presence forever. But the rest of us—all who have been born on this earth—chose to align ourselves with our loving Heavenly Father and His Eternal Son, Jesus Christ.

We must remember that there has been opposition from the beginning of time and that there are two opposing forces operating in the world today—the forces of God the Father and His Son Jesus Christ, and those of Satan, who was cast out of the presence of the Father for rebellion. Satan and his hosts are committed to but one thing—the destruction and deception of God's children. They will use any device and any means, they will employ any tactic, to destroy faith and righteousness in men and women here on earth. (See Revelation 12:7–9; Moses 4:1–4.) Unfortunately, Satan's attack is working all too well. We see evidence every day of the effects of dishonesty, greed, despotism, cruelty, violence, and unabashed immorality.

There is a positive side to this story, however. In the battle fought in the premortal world over the principle of agency, the forces of Jesus Christ were triumphant, and He and our Heavenly Father entered into a covenant with us to do all that was necessary to make it possible for us to one day return to live with them—if we so *choose.* We need not be alone here.

Our Choices Affect the Quality of Our Lives

So we came to earth, a mortal mixture of human frailty and divine potential. While there are few things in this world more needy and dependent than an infant, neither is there anything quite so majestic as the nativity of another child of God. In the words of the poet William Wordsworth in "Ode on Intimations of Immortality":

> *Our birth is but a sleep and a forgetting;*
> *The Soul that rises with us, our life's Star,*
> *Hath had elsewhere its setting*
> *And cometh from afar;*

Not in entire forgetfulness,
And not in utter nakedness,
But trailing clouds of glory do we come
From God, who is our home.

And now we are here, and we are faced with making still more choices—all day, every day. From the moment the alarm goes off in the morning until we set it again at night, we are constantly making decisions—for good and ill. Admittedly, many of those choices are inconsequential. In the eternal scheme of things, it probably doesn't matter much whether or not we have bacon and eggs for breakfast, or whether we choose to ride the bus or drive our car to work. But there are any number of choices we make every day that *are* significant because they affect the quality of our lives.

"The quality of our lives." It's an interesting phrase. I suspect most people think of this concept in terms of the comforts and conveniences they enjoy. But I prefer to think that the quality of our lives has more to do with substance than style. A quality life is one that positively influences others and makes the world around it a better place in which to live. A quality life is one that is constantly growing, expanding its horizons and enlarging its borders. A quality life is one that is filled with love and loyalty, patience and perseverance, kindness and compassion. A quality life is one that is based on eternal potential and not confined to this life only. A quality life is a life well-lived.

But it isn't necessarily a perfect life. Although the Savior set a standard of perfection for all to follow and urged His followers to "be ye therefore perfect, even as your Father which is in heaven is perfect" (Matthew 5:48), He and His Father both understand that, in this mortal life, we humans are often going to fall short of that goal. That's the major reason for Christ's mortal ministry: to give us a way to overcome bad choices when—not if—we make them. The Lord understood in His infinite and eternal wisdom that none of us will live perfectly, and that we will *all* require forgiveness.

Of course, that doesn't justify disobedience to God. As followers of Jesus Christ, we sincerely aspire to follow His example in all things—including the degree of mortal perfection that He attained. But we understand that our realistic objective in this life is to simply do the best we can to obey His commandments. If, during the course of our time here on earth, we learn to use that wondrous gift of agency in positive ways to bless our own lives and the lives of others, then our journey will have been successful—no matter how long it lasts and how much is accomplished.

Coping with Adversity

Not long after my family and I returned home from our mission in Toronto, one of our young missionary friends appeared at our front door unannounced. He had been an outstanding missionary—one of our very strongest leaders—and now he, too, was home. And he was ready to move on with his life.

"President," he said, "do you remember how you made us all promise that when we met someone we wanted to marry, we'd introduce them to you?"

"Yes," I said, smiling, "I remember that."

"Well," he said with great flourish and obvious delight, "I'd like you to meet my fiancée!"

He introduced us to a wonderful young woman, and we spent a few minutes getting acquainted. It quickly became clear that she was every bit as faithful and strong as he. What a wonderful couple they made—so sweet, so pure, so very much in love. I was honored when they asked me to perform their temple marriage, which was scheduled to take place about three months in the future. We put a circle around that date on the calendar, and then I bade the young couple goodnight.

The next evening I received a telephone call with news that shocked me to the very soul. The young missionary who'd stood in my living room with his fiancée the night before had been killed in an automobile accident. Instead of officiating at his wedding, I was being asked to speak at his funeral.

For those whose understanding is limited to the confines of mortality, death can sometimes appear to be terribly cruel and capricious. Indeed, life itself is filled with harsh realities that tug at the heart and tear away at the soul. Child abuse. AIDS. Natural disasters, from hurricanes to earthquakes. Famine. Prejudice and intolerance. Humanity's ongoing inhumanity toward one another.

One cannot look at human suffering, regardless of its causes or origins, and not feel pain and compassion. It is easy to understand why one who lacks an eternal perspective might look at horrifying news footage of starving children in Africa or the devastation of a hurricane and shake a fist at the heavens.

"If there is a God," the empathetic observer might wonder, "how could He allow such things to happen?"

The answer isn't easy, but it isn't that complicated, either. God has put His plan into motion. It proceeds through natural laws—which are, in fact, *God's* laws. And because they are His, He is bound by them, as are we. In this imperfect world, bad things sometimes happen. The earth's rocky underpinnings occasionally slip and slide, and earthquakes result. Certain weather patterns turn into hurricanes, tornadoes, floods, and drought. That is the nature of our existence on this planet. Dealing with adversity is one of the chief ways in which we are tested and tutored.

Sometimes, however, adversity is man-made. That is where the principle of agency again comes into play. Keep in mind that we were so excited about the plan Heavenly Father and Jesus Christ presented that we literally "shouted for joy." (Job 38:7.) We loved the concept of mortality and the exciting notion of moral agency. But because we'd never been mortal before, I'm not sure we could fully comprehend the impact of agency on our lives.

We tend to think of agency in a personal way. Ask someone to define "moral agency" and they'll probably come up with something like this: "Moral agency means I'm free to make choices for myself." But we forget that agency also offers that same privilege to others, which means that sometimes we are going to be adversely affected by the way other people choose to exercise their agency.

Heavenly Father feels so strongly about protecting our moral agency that He will allow all of His children to exercise it—for good and for evil. Of course, He has an eternal perspective that helps Him to understand that whatever pain and suffering we endure in this life, regardless of its origins and causes, it is only a moment compared with our entire eternal existence.

By way of illustration, let's say you had a rope that extended both directions off into the cosmos—forever. And let's say you took a single strand of thread and wrapped it around the rope once at its midpoint. The rope to the left of the thread could represent our life before birth. The rope to the right of the thread could represent our life after death. And that single strand of thread would represent the span of our mortal lives here on earth in comparison to eternity.

Sort of puts it in perspective, doesn't it?

Of course, we mortals can rarely view life from that perspective. Instead, we feel pain and anguish in the face of adversity—for ourselves and for others. But faith in our Heavenly Father and in His plan can be a source of inner strength through which we can find peace, comfort, and the courage to cope. As we put our faith and trust to work, hope is born. Hope grows out of faith and gives meaning and purpose to all that we do. It can give us comfort in the face of adversity, strength in times of trial, and peace when there is every reason for doubt and anguish.

I felt that comfort, strength, and peace as I stood before the huge congregation that had gathered for my young missionary's funeral. As I looked into the faces of his family, fiancée, and friends, I felt the comfort that comes through knowing and accepting God's eternal plan. Although we would all miss him, we shared in the knowledge that life is eternal and that my missionary would be separated from us for only a season. One day, we knew, we could all be together in God's kingdom—if we chose to live as well and faithfully as he did.

Thus illuminated by the light of faith, adversity becomes a vehicle for growth and death becomes a doorway from one phase of our eternal existence to another.

There Is Life after Death

Several years ago my father died. Within a year my mother also passed away. While neither death was completely unexpected, it was still hard to say good-bye to both of my parents—especially just ten months apart. How grateful I was then—and am now—for the sweet assurance that God has a plan for us extending beyond the here and now, that our lives here have a great purpose and are an important preparation for what lies ahead. What a blessing it is to know that death is not an end, that there is a glorious reward in store for those who learn to make good choices in this life, and that our most treasured relationships can extend beyond mortality and throughout eternity.

Of course, we don't know everything about what lies beyond death. The Savior indicated that His Father's House has "many mansions" (John 14:2), which seems to imply that the next world consists of more than one destination.

Latter-day revelation teaches us that we will all be assigned to one of three eternal kingdoms, or degrees of glory, depending upon our faithfulness in this life (see D&C 76). Heavenly Father and Jesus Christ live in the highest degree of glory, or the celestial kingdom. Those who are worthy to be exalted in this kingdom not only receive the privilege of living forever in the presence of God and Christ, but they also become "heirs of God, and joint-heirs with Christ" (Romans 8:17) of all that the Father has and is.

In other words, each of us has within us the potential to become like our Eternal Father.

Now, I realize that may sound pretentious to some. But there is no pretense in that doctrine—only wonder, awe, and profound gratitude for a kind and loving Father in Heaven who has, in his infinite love and wisdom, created a plan whereby we may become like Him and His Son, Jesus Christ. Please understand that in no way does this denigrate our Heavenly Father's supreme role in our eternal lives. He is and always will be our Father and our God. But like any benevolent father, He wants the best for His children. He wants us to be happy. He wants us to succeed. And so He wants us to be like Him.

How exactly does that happen? Through a Book of Mormon prophet named Alma we know that we will move through the eternities with a glorified and, yes, *perfected* physical body. As we read earlier, Alma taught that Christ made possible the resurrection of the dead, which means that "the spirit and the body shall be reunited again in its perfect form; both limb and joint shall be restored to its proper frame, even as we now are at this time. . . . And even there shall not so much as a hair of their heads be lost; but every thing shall be restored to its perfect frame." (Alma 11:43–44.)

As to the process of becoming *spiritually* perfect "even as [our] Father which is in Heaven is perfect," well, that's the part we don't know a lot about. Certainly the experiences and opportunities of earth life have a great deal to do with it. All of us came here with the personal responsibility to seek for God's eternal truth, to abide by it, and yes, to share it with others when we find it. The Apostle Paul taught his listeners in Athens "that they should *seek the Lord,* if haply they might *feel after him,* and find him, though he be not far from every one of us: For in him we live, and move, and have our being; as certain also of your own poets have said, *For we are also his offspring."* (Acts 17:27–28; emphasis added; see also 2 Peter 1:4 and 1 John 3:1–2.)

Additionally, there is scriptural evidence to suggest that our spiritual growth will continue in the next life. Peter taught that after Jesus Christ died He "went and preached unto the spirits in prison." (1 Peter 3:19.) Now, why would the Savior do a thing like that unless there was a chance for spiritual growth among those to whom He was preaching?

Added Peter: "For for this cause was the gospel preached also to them that are dead, that they might be judged according to men in the flesh, but live according to God in the spirit." (1 Peter 4:6.)

Of course, Peter was teaching the same doctrine he had heard the Savior Himself teach: "Verily, verily, I say unto you, The hour is coming, and now is, when the dead shall hear the voice of the Son of God: and they that hear shall live." (John 5:25.)

Clearly, Jesus and His disciples understood that Heavenly Father's plan included eternal opportunities for spiritual progression. But beyond that, we don't have many specifics about the next phase of our eternal lives. That's where our faith comes in. We know that God has promised incredible blessings to those who learn in this life to walk by faith and exercise the moral agency He has given us to make good decisions and choices (including, it should be noted, the choice we all have to believe this eternal plan or not to believe it). That should be enough. We don't have to know all of the details of those promised blessings. We just have to have confidence in them. And faith in Him.

Which shouldn't be all that difficult, when you think about it. After all that our Heavenly Father has done to create this incredible plan for us—from the miracle of birth to the miracle of Eternal Life in the presence of God and the Savior—it is clear to see how deeply He loves each one of us, and how much He wants us to be eternally happy with Him. And that should make it easy for all of us to trust in Him.

The Articles of Faith

About twelve years after The Church of Jesus Christ of Latter-day Saints was organized, the editor of *The Chicago Democrat* asked Joseph Smith to prepare an article for publication detailing Church history and beliefs. The article was significant because it included the first simple, concise declaration of Latter-day Saint doctrine from the perspective of the Church's founder, a prophet of God. Since that time, the points enumerated by Joseph Smith in newsprint have come to be known as the Articles of Faith.

Within these thirteen articles, or statements of belief, are found the essence of LDS theology. We have already talked about many of these beliefs in earlier chapters, so we won't spend much more time with them here. But let's look at the Articles so that you can get a sense of the broad doctrinal expanse they embrace.

The Godhead

1. *We believe in God, the Eternal Father, and in His Son, Jesus Christ, and in the Holy Ghost.*

Because of some of the things we've already covered, you probably have a good idea about our concept of Heavenly Father and the Savior, Jesus Christ. Our feelings about them run deep and are richly personal. God is indeed our

Heavenly Father, with all of the warmth, tenderness, and caring that the word *father* should imply. Similarly, while Jesus is our Lord and Master, full of majesty and glory, He is also God's firstborn spirit Son, and therefore our Brother. His love for us is therefore familial and personal, as is our love for Him.

Our message to the world is that there is a kind and loving God in Heaven who sent His Only Begotten Son, Jesus Christ, to earth to teach His gospel, organize His Church, and atone for the sins of the world—not necessarily in that order. This is the Ultimate Truth around which all other truth revolves.

The third member of the Godhead, the Holy Ghost—sometimes called the Holy Spirit, the Spirit of God, the Spirit of the Lord, or the Comforter—has a magnificent mission, one unique aspect of which is to testify of truth, particularly as it relates to the Father and the Son. If we believe in God with all our hearts, it is only because that significant truth has been confirmed upon our souls through the power of the Holy Ghost. If we love the Lord, it is because the Holy Ghost has moved upon us and spiritually introduced us to His eternal reality and condescending grace. And if you have felt warm, positive feelings as you have read this book, it is because the Holy Ghost is confirming my testimony and telling you that what I have written is true.

Almost everyone has felt the influence of the Holy Ghost at some point in life. It is through the Holy Ghost that truth is confirmed upon our souls. But the special ministry of the Holy Ghost is to help people believe and follow the teachings of the Father and the Son. In order to accomplish this important mission, he must be different from the other members of the Godhead in at least one respect. Through Joseph Smith the Lord revealed that "the Father has a body of flesh and bones as tangible as man's; the Son also; but the Holy Ghost has not a body of flesh and bones, but is a personage of Spirit. Were it not so, the Holy Ghost could not dwell in us." (D&C 130:22.)

As noted earlier, moral agency is the key ingredient in Heavenly Father's plan for our eternal progression. Heavenly Father and Jesus gave us the right to choose; the Holy Ghost is available to all of us to help us make correct choices—if we choose to listen.

My father was in the automobile business and I followed the same profession early in my business career. One day the Ford Motor Company came to town searching for a dealer to represent a magnificent new automobile line they were about to introduce that they were sure was going to revolutionize the industry. This car was going to be so great that Henry Ford II planned to name it in honor of his father. So the Ford people were anxious to find the right local representative for this line of cars, and they visited me often to talk about it. I've got to tell you, they were very persuasive.

I struggled with the decision of whether or not to become their dealer. We were doing quite well with the lines we were then representing, and I was afraid of undoing a good thing. But if this new line was even half of what Ford was claiming it would be, I would be passing up the business opportunity of a lifetime if I turned them down.

I prayed for guidance. Now, you might wonder if it's appropriate to ask God to help you make decisions about business affairs and investments. But I believe the words of the Book of Mormon prophet Amulek, who taught: "Cry unto [God] over the crops of your fields, that ye may prosper in them. Cry over the flocks of your fields, that they may increase. . . . Yea, and when you do not cry unto the Lord, let your hearts be full, drawn out in prayer unto him continually for your welfare, and also for the welfare of those who are around you." (Alma 34:24–27.)

So I asked Heavenly Father to help me make this important business decision. And He did. When my father and I saw the car for the first time I had the clear impression: "Do not sign the franchise." At that moment there was no doubt in my mind that it would be the wrong thing for me to do.

But Ford didn't ask me to sign the franchise right away. They allowed me time to think about it, and then they started to sell me again. I'm sorry to admit that I eventually succumbed to their sales pressure, ignored the promptings that I had been praying to receive, and signed the franchise agreement to become Salt Lake City's first Edsel dealer. If you know your automotive history, you know that I was also the city's *last* Edsel dealer, because the car turned out to be one of the biggest failures in industry history. Not only did Ford lose hundreds of millions of dollars in the campaign, but all of their Edsel dealers incurred huge losses—including me. It was without a doubt the darkest period of my professional business career.

And it could have been avoided—for me, anyway—if I had just listened to the whisperings of the Holy Ghost. That's the funny thing about that situation. I had prayed and asked for guidance, and I had received the Lord's counsel through the Holy Spirit, clearly and unmistakably. Yet I still decided to go against that spiritual prompting, and my family and I suffered as a consequence.

Thankfully, that experience and others have taught me the importance of responding to the prompting of the Spirit when it speaks. I have had rich and rewarding experiences too numerous to mention as a result of following that direction. I know I couldn't fulfill my present assignment as an Apostle of the Lord Jesus Christ without the guidance, comfort, and sustaining influence of the third member of the Godhead, the Holy Ghost.

Personal Accountability

2. *We believe that men will be punished for their own sins, and not for Adam's transgression.*

The second article of faith has reference to the traditional Christian concept of Original Sin, which claims that because of the fall of Adam and Eve in the Garden of Eden we are all born into this world as sinners. The Church of Jesus Christ of Latter-day Saints discounts the notion of Original Sin and its ascribed negative impact on humanity. Indeed, we honor and respect Adam and Eve for their wisdom and foresight. Their lives in the Garden of Eden were blissful and pleasant; choosing to leave that behind so they and the entire human family could experience both the triumphs and travails of mortality must not have been easy. But we believe that they *did* choose mortality, and in so doing made it possible for all of us to participate in Heavenly Father's great, eternal plan.

While it's true that all of us who share space on this planet have made mistakes in our lives at one time or another, we believe that we are not *born* sinners. Indeed, the Book of Mormon prophet Mormon taught his son Moroni that "little children are alive in Christ, even from the foundation of the world." (Moroni 8:12.)

In other words, we're born good; we learn to sin as we grow older. And if you need evidence of the truth of that doctrine, please see your nearest infant. Look deeply into the child's eyes. Have you ever seen such sweetness and purity? It's like you can look through a baby's eyes right into heaven.

Of course, that changes a little later in their lives when wide-eyed innocence turns into wild-eyed mischievousness. That's when children become accountable and capable of sin—when they know and understand the difference between right and wrong. Through the Prophet Joseph Smith the Lord revealed that the age of accountability is eight years old. It is the responsibility of parents to teach their children to understand the doctrines of the kingdom and to prepare them for the eternal responsibility of accountability.

And as for "Adam's transgression," well, there's no need

to worry. You're not any more accountable for his mistakes than he is for yours. That's part of the principle of moral agency—everyone makes his or her own choices and is singularly responsible for the consequences of those decisions. While it's true that we are all affected by the way in which others, including Adam, choose to use their agency, we are only held accountable for the decisions we make ourselves. The rest we just have to deal with the best we can—which is either good or bad news, depending on our skill as decision-makers.

The Atonement

3. *We believe that through the Atonement of Christ, all mankind may be saved, by obedience to the laws and ordinances of the Gospel.*

There is no more wonderful doctrine in all of Christianity than the doctrine of the Atonement. I think about it—and thank God for it—every day of my life. Although we've already considered the Savior's benevolence elsewhere within these pages, there is one aspect of this doctrine that deserves more illumination.

Jesus Christ accomplished two incomparable feats through His atoning sacrifice. First, He conquered death, and as a result all people will have the privilege of everlasting life with a resurrected body. Second, He suffered the burden and pains of our sins so that we might have the privilege of eternal life in the presence of God if we have faith in Christ as our Savior and choose to repent of our sins and keep His commandments. The first—salvation from the bonds of death—is given to all of us freely. There is nothing we can do to receive it. It is a gift to us provided through the loving grace of Jesus Christ. The second—exaltation in God's celestial kingdom—requires effort on our part to believe, repent, and be "doers of the word, and not hearers only." (James 1:22.)

Thus we believe the teaching of the Book of Mormon prophet Nephi that "it is by grace that we are saved, after all we can do." (2 Nephi 25:23.) But we also understand what John the Revelator was talking about when, within his prophetic vision, he "saw the dead, small and great, stand before God; and the books were opened: and another book was opened, which is the book of life: and the dead were judged out of those things which were written in the books, according to their works." (Revelation 20:12.)

Of course, no matter what we do we must never forget that both gifts—salvation and exaltation—are available to us only in and through our Savior, Jesus Christ. And an interesting thing happens when we take full advantage of the Atonement's promises for a joyful eternity. Those who repent and "come unto Christ" (Moroni 10:32) discover in exciting ways that they can more easily cope with the challenges of mortality as well.

"Come unto me, all ye that labour and are heavy laden," the Savior said, "and I will give you rest.

"Take my yoke upon you, and learn of me; for I am meek and lowly in heart: and ye shall find rest unto your souls.

"For my yoke is easy, and my burden is light." (Matthew 11:28–30.)

Thus the Atonement is a principle of comfort and strength through trial and adversity to all who embrace its powerful influence—in this life and forever.

The First Principles of the Gospel

4. *We believe that the first principles and ordinances of the Gospel are: first, Faith in the Lord Jesus Christ; second, Repentance; third, Baptism by immersion for the remission of sins; fourth, Laying on of hands for the gift of the Holy Ghost.*

Faith in Christ and repentance through His Atonement are the very foundation of the gospel as taught by The Church of Jesus Christ of Latter-day Saints. But what about baptism?

A latter-day Apostle, James E. Talmage, defined baptism as "the gateway leading into the fold of Christ, the portal to the Church, the established rite of naturalization in the kingdom of God." (*The Articles of Faith* [Salt Lake City: Deseret Book, 1913], page 120.) Through baptism we take upon ourselves the name of Christ and promise to do the things that He would do, including obeying God's commandments. In return, the Lord promises to send His spirit to guide, strengthen, and comfort us. Perhaps most importantly, He also promises to forgive us of our sins for which we truly repent. In a very literal way, those who go down into the waters of baptism have their sins washed away. They emerge from the baptismal font as sin-free and clean as the day they were born.

Alma, a Book of Mormon prophet, gave this invitation to his people: "Come and be baptized unto repentance, that ye may be washed from your sins, that ye may have faith on the Lamb of God, who taketh away the sins of the world, who is mighty to save and to cleanse from all unrighteousness.

"Yea, I say unto you come and fear not, and lay aside every sin, which easily doth beset you, which doth bind you down to destruction, yea, come and go forth, and show unto your God that ye are willing to repent of your sins and enter into a covenant with him to keep his commandments, and witness it unto him this day by going into the waters of baptism." (Alma 7:14–15.)

Jesus, of course, set the example for us in this regard during His journey through mortality. The scriptures record that before He began His three-year ministry, He sought His cousin, John, who held priesthood authority to baptize.

"But John forbad him, saying, I have need to be baptized of thee, and comest thou to me?

"And Jesus answering said unto him, Suffer it to be so now: for thus it becometh us to fulfil all righteousness. Then he suffered him.

"And Jesus, when he was baptized, went up straightway out of the water: and, lo, the heavens were opened unto him, and he saw the Spirit of God descending like a dove, and lighting upon him:

"And lo a voice from heaven, saying, This is my beloved Son, in whom I am well pleased." (Matthew 3:14–17.)

Of course, Jesus didn't need to be baptized for a remission of His sins, as He alone had lived a sinless life. But the Book of Mormon prophet Nephi explained that the Savior "showeth unto the children of men that, according to the flesh he humbleth himself before the Father, and witnesseth unto the Father that he would be obedient unto him in keeping his commandments." (2 Nephi 31:7.)

As in all things, it is the greatest desire of Latter-day Saints to follow the example Jesus set, which is why we believe in the essential ordinance of baptism by immersion for the remission of sin.

Soon after one is baptized, worthy men holding priesthood authority place their hands upon the head of the just-baptized individual to confirm him or her a member of The Church of Jesus Christ of Latter-day Saints and to bestow a very special gift: the gift of the Holy Ghost. While almost every person on this planet will at least occasionally feel the Holy Ghost prompting them toward truth, those who have shown their desire to follow and serve the Lord through baptism and have received the gift of the Holy Ghost by the laying on of hands are *entitled* to the guidance of the Holy Spirit. As they live worthily they will receive spiritual direction which, if they choose to follow it, will lead them safely home to Heavenly Father.

The gift of the Holy Ghost intensifies our relationship with that member of the Godhead. In a way, it's like living next door to the fire house. Although everyone is entitled to fire department services, the safest person in town is the one who lives next door to the fire station. And that's what the gift of the Holy Ghost does—it makes him a part of our lives. It introduces the third member of the Godhead into our hearts and souls and puts him on duty in our lives—a tremendous advantage, to be sure, but only as long as we're willing to pay attention to his whisperings and promptings.

Priesthood Authority

5. *We believe that a man must be called of God, by prophecy, and by the laying on of hands by those who are in authority, to preach the Gospel and administer in the ordinances thereof.*

As noted in our earlier discussion of priesthood authority, the priesthood is God's authority given to humans to do the things that He and the Savior would do if they were here living among us. It is the conduit through which Heavenly Father governs His children in an orderly, nonoppressive way.

Priesthood government differs drastically from any other government. Whereas all too often human government is based in revolution and driven by might, priesthood government is based in revelation and driven by the Almighty. And while the heart and soul of mortal government is the law, created by lawmakers who have various capabilities and motivations, at the heart of priesthood government are the commandments of God, created by a kind and loving Father in Heaven of infinite capability, whose only motivation is our eternal success.

And when it comes right down to it, that's the only motivation of priesthood authority: to assist in bringing Heavenly Father's children safely home to Him.

The Church of Jesus Christ

6. *We believe in the same organization that existed in the Primitive Church, namely, apostles, prophets, pastors, teachers, evangelists, and so forth.*

For some, the idea that Jesus organized a church while He was here on the earth is new and perhaps a little disconcerting. But it's clear that He did. Paul indicates that Jesus "gave some, apostles; and some, prophets; and some, evangelists; and some, pastors and teachers." (Ephesians 4:11.)

And why did he do this?

"For the perfecting of the saints, for the work of the ministry, for the edifying of the body of Christ:

"Till we all come in the unity of the faith, and of the knowledge of the Son of God, unto a perfect man, unto the measure of the stature of the fulness of Christ;

"That we henceforth be no more children, tossed to and fro, and carried about with every wind of doctrine, by the sleight of men, and cunning craftiness, whereby they lie in wait to deceive." (Ephesians 4:12–14.)

As indicated previously, the church that Jesus Christ organized during His mortal ministry was unable to survive in its entirety beyond the first century following his death and resurrection in Jerusalem. That's why Peter prophesied that there would need to be a "restitution of all things" (Acts 3:21)—including the organization of Christ's Church. And we believe that restitution, or restoration, took place through the Prophet Joseph Smith, and that The Church of Jesus Christ of Latter-day Saints is, indeed, Christ's Church on earth, with a living prophet at its head and an inspired quorum of Twelve Apostles. It is in very fact the Church of Jesus Christ.

And what a blessing this is in the lives of those who believe in and follow these living prophets and apostles! Knowing that there is a prophet of God on earth today doesn't relieve Latter-day Saints from the burden of thinking and acting for themselves. We all have the responsibility to respond to the whisperings of the Holy Spirit in our own lives. But the inspired counsel of God's chosen servants provides those who pay attention with an extra source of spiritual strength and insight. The principles of the gospel are clarified and the plan of salvation is explained so that all may know how to live in accordance with the Lord's teachings.

93

Those who have access to latter-day revelation through living prophets and apostles face life's most demanding tests more confidently, because they know to whom they can turn to find the truth.

Spiritual Gifts

7. We believe in the gift of tongues, prophecy, revelation, visions, healing, interpretation of tongues, and so forth.

It is our testimony to the world that the spiritual gifts that existed in such rich abundance during the time of Christ and His holy Apostles are again active and vibrant in the lives of God's children today. According to the Savior, these spiritual gifts "are given for the benefit of those who love me and keep all my commandments, and him that seeketh so to do; that all may be benefitted." (D&C 46:9.)

We have missionaries throughout the world who have experienced the gift of tongues that they might teach the gospel in its fulness to people who speak a different language. We have prophets who receive revelation from God—even visions—that they might communicate the will of the Father to His children. And we have miracles of healing wrought through the power of faith and the authority of the priesthood "that all may be benefitted."

"And all these gifts come from God," the Lord told Joseph Smith, "for the benefit of the children of God." (D&C 46:26.)

Several years ago I was sitting at my desk when I suddenly felt that I needed to go to a nearby hospital to see a neighbor who had been admitted with a heart problem. At first I thought I would stop by on my way home from work, as there had been no indication that my friend's condition was serious. But the spiritual prompting was strong: I must go immediately. By this time in my life I had learned to respond to the whisperings of the Holy Spirit, so I went, though I didn't know exactly why.

When I arrived at the hospital, I was told that my friend

THE ARTICLES OF FAITH

had suffered a major heart attack. Even though he was alone in his room and seemed to be asleep, I felt I should give him a blessing of health and total recovery. So I placed my hands upon his head and blessed him through the authority of the priesthood.

I have since learned that my neighbor's vital signs began changing soon after I gave him the blessing. Within five days he was out of the hospital, and he experienced a remarkable recovery within a month.

"It has been eight years now," my friend wrote recently. "Today I still work eight to ten hours a day. I play golf. I walk each day. I even water ski. And I never forget that by all accounts I should be dead. Thank you for these last eight years. And thank God!"

Is the age of miracles over? Not by a long shot. God continues to do miraculous things among His children through the gifts of the Spirit.

The Bible and the Book of Mormon

8. *We believe the Bible to be the word of God as far as it is translated correctly; we also believe the Book of Mormon to be the word of God.*

As discussed earlier, Latter-day Saints love and honor the Holy Bible as the word of God. We read it, we study it, and we teach from it. Our lives are enriched by the powerful stories and messages of the Old and New Testaments.

However, we are also aware that the Bible has been through countless translations from the time its chapters were originally penned to the present. Along the way there have been changes and alterations that have diminished the purity of the doctrine. While it is indeed a miracle that the Bible has survived through the ages at all, it would be unreasonable to assume that it has done so completely intact.

That is why members of The Church of Jesus Christ of Latter-day Saints are so thankful for the additional insights, revelations, and inspiration contained in the Book of Mormon, Doctrine and Covenants, and the Pearl of Great Price. These scriptural volumes confirm Bible truths while expanding doctrinal horizons beyond biblical boundaries. And they do so while adding additional witnesses to the Bible's testimony that God lives, that Jesus is the Christ, and that they love us enough to prepare a way for all of us to return to live with them in happiness and peace.

Modern-day Revelation

9. *We believe all that God has revealed, all that He does now reveal, and we believe that He will yet reveal many great and important things pertaining to the Kingdom of God.*

Among the most wondrous of all the gifts of the Spirit is the gift of revelation. As the Old Testament prophet Amos declared, "Surely the Lord God will do nothing, but he revealeth his secret unto his servants the prophets." (Amos 3:7.) As one who has had the privilege of knowing and associating with God's living prophets, I humbly testify that the heavens are not sealed. While there have been times during the earth's history when, because of apostasy and unbelief, the Lord's church has not been present upon the earth and therefore revelation to and through chosen prophets has ceased for a time, that is not the case in our day. The gospel of Jesus Christ has been restored, and God continues to reveal His will through men whom He has called to be His representatives on earth.

It is important to understand that *God* never sealed the heavens in the first place; man did. It was man who proclaimed that there would be no more revelation, that God had said all He had to say. Yet how presumptuous for man to tell God that He can't speak to His children! Indeed, as we discussed earlier, Heavenly Father spoke to a fourteen-year-old boy who approached him in simple, earnest prayer and who clearly *believed* that He would respond. I take comfort in knowing that God loves His children today as much as He loved those in ancient times who had the blessing and benefit of prophetic direction.

But God doesn't speak only to those who have been called to be prophets and revelators. You and I can receive personal revelation for our own lives and for our families and personal responsibilities if we will live in such a way that we can be open and receptive to the whisperings of the Holy Spirit when they come. Said the Lord through the Prophet Nephi: "I will give unto the children of men line upon line, precept upon precept, here a little and there a little; and blessed are those who hearken unto my precepts, and lend an ear unto my counsel, for they shall learn wisdom; for unto him that receiveth I will give more; and from them that shall say, We have enough, from them shall be taken away even that which they have." (2 Nephi 28:30.)

The Gathering of Israel

10. *We believe in the literal gathering of Israel and in the restoration of the Ten Tribes; that Zion (the New Jerusalem) will be built upon the American continent; that Christ will reign personally upon the earth; and, that the earth will be renewed and receive its paradisiacal glory.*

The tenth article of faith has to do with the prophetic destiny of the American continent and Christ's foretold millennial reign upon the earth. It affirms every scriptural prophecy regarding the second coming of Christ, including biblical prophecies relative to the gathering of Israel and the return of the Ten Tribes of Israel that became "lost" when the invading Assyrians deported them around 722 B.C. It is not my purpose here to explain such detailed doctrine. It suffices to say we believe that all that has been prophesied by God's prophets will eventually come to pass, and that Jesus Christ will return to earth in power and majesty to rule as King of Kings in reclaiming His people and ushering in a millennial era of peace.

Of course, some find that prospect rather frightening. After all, those prophecies include promises of trouble, trauma, and tragedy all around the world. And while I freely acknowledge the difficulties that surely will come, there is peace in knowing that the Lord is in control. He knows the end from the beginning. He has given us adequate instruction that, if followed, will see us safely through any crisis. His purposes will be fulfilled, and someday we will understand. For now, however, we must be careful not to overreact to our concerns, nor should we be caught up in extreme preparations. What we must do is keep the commandments of God and never lose hope.

"Fear not, little flock," said the Lord through Joseph Smith, "do good; let earth and hell combine against you, for if ye are built upon my rock, they cannot prevail. . . . Look unto me in every thought; doubt not, fear not." (D&C 6:34, 36.)

Worshiping God

11. *We claim the privilege of worshiping Almighty God according to the dictates of our own conscience, and allow all men the same privilege, let them worship how, where or what they may.*

Given the history of persecution that members of our church have endured, it's easy to understand why the principle of religious tolerance is very important to us. But just as important as claiming this privilege for ourselves is the responsibility of all Latter-day Saints to preserve and protect this right for others—which means we may occasionally have to stand up for someone else's right to a religious practice with which we don't necessarily agree. But when it comes right down to it, religious tolerance doesn't really have to do with commonality and shared beliefs; it has to do with getting along with each other despite our deepest differences, and working to protect one another's right to those differences.

This might logically lead you to wonder why we Latter-day Saints expend so much energy in trying to convert others to our way of thinking and worshiping. Please understand that it isn't because we don't believe others have a right to worship as they choose, because they most certainly do. But part of what we believe includes a divine commission to share our faith—and the joy and peace we have found within it—with others.

"And I give unto you a commandment that you shall teach one another the doctrine of the kingdom," the Lord said through the Prophet Joseph Smith.

"Teach ye diligently and my grace shall attend you, that you may be instructed more perfectly in theory, in principle, in doctrine, in the law of the gospel, in all things that pertain unto the kingdom of God, that are expedient for you to understand;

"Of things both in heaven and in the earth, and under the earth; things which have been, things which are, things which must shortly come to pass; things which are at home, things which are abroad; the wars and the perplexities of the nations, and the judgments which are on the land; and a knowledge also of countries and of kingdoms—

"Behold, I sent you out to testify and warn the people, and it becometh every man who hath been warned to warn his neighbor." (D&C 88:77–79, 81.)

And so we share our beliefs as a voice of warning to all people, and invite them to "come unto Christ, and be perfected in him." (Moroni 10:32.) But as always, it's up to them whether they choose to respond to that warning and invitation.

Honoring the Law

12. *We believe in being subject to kings, presidents, rulers, and magistrates, in obeying, honoring, and sustaining the law.*

Patriotism has always been important to Latter-day Saints, regardless of nationality or political philosophy. In 1835 Joseph

Smith declared, "We believe that governments were instituted of God for the benefit of man; and that he holds men accountable for their acts in relation to them, both in making laws and administering them, for the good and safety of society." (D&C 134:1.) Today Latter-day Saints live in nearly every nation of the world, and function under almost every governmental regime imaginable. But for all, that declaration remains true: "We believe in . . . obeying, honoring, and sustaining the law."

Christlike Virtues

13. *We believe in being honest, true, chaste, benevolent, virtuous, and in doing good to all men; indeed, we may say that we follow the admonition of Paul—We believe all things, we hope all things, we have endured many things, and hope to be able to endure all things. If there is anything virtuous, lovely, or of good report or praiseworthy, we seek after these things.*

With this eloquent statement of sincere Christian belief Joseph Smith concluded the Articles of Faith, which in total comprise a powerful articulation of the practical religion that Latter-day Saints embrace and attempt to practice. It is positive and upbeat. It looks outward and upward. More than anything else, it is hopeful.

Hope is a precious principle by which to live. Hope grows out of faith and gives meaning and purpose to all that we do. It can even give us the peaceful assurance we need to live happily in a world that is ripe with iniquity, calamity, and injustice.

As the end of the Savior's mortal ministry drew near, He offered this reassuring hope to His beloved disciples: "Peace I leave with you, my peace I give unto you: not as the world giveth, give I unto you. Let not your heart be troubled, neither let it be afraid." (John 14:27.)

That is the hope we cling to, as articulated by the Prophet Joseph Smith in the Articles of Faith. And the peace it promises to all mankind is the "peace of God, which passeth all understanding." (Philippians 4:7.)

Fruits of Living the Gospel

CHAPTER EIGHT

In 1969 I traveled to Mexico with three business associates. All three were outstanding businessmen, and each had amassed a considerable fortune; in fact, one was widely reported to be one of the richest men in the entire world. The four of us sat together in the lavish executive compartment of a private jet—a billionaire, two millionaires.

And me.

As we flew to Mexico these three wealthy executives discussed multimillion dollar business deals like other people discuss last night's ball game or recent movies they've seen. To tell you the truth, I was intimidated—especially when the billionaire turned to me and asked, "So tell me, Ballard, what exactly is it that you do?"

"After listening to the three of you talk," I said, "I guess I don't do very much at all."

They chuckled at my comment. But none of them seemed to disagree with my assessment of the situation.

As our conversation continued, however, it became clear that, although these were men of good will who had done many good things in the world with their wealth, the most important thing in life to the billionaire was to accumulate more and more money, which appeared to be the source of his power and prestige. Wealth seemed to be what made him happy and proud. As far as I could tell, it was his passion, his obsession, his very reason for being. As he discussed his international financial empire and impressive array of worldly possessions, I sensed that beneath that collection of materialism was a foundation of unhappiness that comes from spiritual deprivation. The billionaire did not speak joyfully of family or friends. He seemed not to know much of real peace or contentment. The gospel of Jesus Christ was not part of his life. In a contemplative moment he said to me, "I'm not sure there is such a thing as life after one dies. But if there is, I wonder if any of this will matter much."

Obviously, neither option—death as the ultimate end of existence or life beyond the grave without worldly acclaim or accumulation—gave him much comfort.

Happiness Is the Greatest of All Riches

When I returned home a couple of days later my wife, Barbara, met me at the airport and we returned to our comfortable home in Salt Lake City. When she asked me how I had enjoyed my sampling of life in the fastest of all financial fast lanes, I could only sigh and respond, "Honey, we may not have much money or the other things that some people think are so important. But I have a feeling that of the four men on that plane, I was the happiest and, in a way, the richest. I have blessings that money simply cannot buy. And I have the satisfaction of knowing that the things that are most important to me—you, our family, and my love of God—can endure forever."

I couldn't help but think of the Savior's words to His disciples when He said, "Lay not up for yourselves treasures upon the earth, where moth and rust doth corrupt, and where thieves break through and steal:

"But lay up for yourselves treasures in heaven, where

neither moth nor rust doth corrupt, and where thieves do not break through nor steal:

"For where your treasure is, there will your heart be also." (Matthew 6:19–21.)

Finding Peace in a Troubled World

The treasure we're talking about is a feeling of comfort, peace, and eternal security. Because I know that I'm part of a holy plan designed by a Heavenly Father who loves all of His children equally and who wants them all to achieve eternal success, there's no pressure on me to compete with anyone for worldly acclaim and accomplishment. Please don't misunderstand: There are many good men and women in the Church of considerable means who know and live Heavenly Father's eternal plan. Their contributions to God's kingdom, both spiritually and financially, have been significant. We all want to provide the necessities of life for our families and do the best we can with the talents God has given us. But when considered from the unique perspective of eternity, fame and popularity aren't nearly as important as loving and being loved; status doesn't mean much when compared to service; and acquiring spiritual knowledge is infinitely more meaningful than acquiring an excess of wealth.

It's that perspective and the attendant spiritual and emotional tranquillity that are among the positive fruits of knowing—*really* knowing and living the gospel of Jesus Christ. It clarifies the relationship between people and their God and gives meaning and purpose to every individual life. Far more than being just another way of worshiping, it is a way of life. It guides every decision and underscores every relationship, including one's relationship with oneself. You see, you can never look at yourself in the same way if you know that you are a child of God, and that He knows you, loves you, and cares about you. And you can never look at others dispassionately if you know that they are your eternal brothers and sisters who, like you, are here on earth trying to learn and grow through mortal experiences, both good and bad.

In a world teeming with uncertainty and frustration, such understanding brings a peace of mind that is a delicious gospel fruit, indeed. What comfort and security come from knowing that we have a purpose for being! What a blessing to have the solid anchor of specific values by which to live! How exciting to understand our ultimate, divine potential! How reassuring to realize there is a source of power much greater than our own, which can be accessed through personal faith and prayer and through the righteous exercise of God's priesthood authority! And how encouraging to know that there is a source of strength that can help us cope with daily trials and find peace in a troubled, turbulent world!

Of course, there are other tangible, recognizable fruits. Because our Heavenly Father knows, loves, and understands us, He has built into gospel living countless ways to bless and strengthen us as individuals and as families. These fruits include, but are not limited to, the following:

The Word of Wisdom: Being Happy, Healthy, and Wise

If you know anything about The Church of Jesus Christ of Latter-day Saints, you probably know that its faithful members don't smoke, drink alcoholic beverages, or consume coffee or tea. You may have even admired the Church for responding so resolutely to the ever-increasing body of scientific evidence indicating how dangerous all of these substances are. But the fact is that that instruction was originally given to the Church in 1833, the result of a revelation given to the Prophet Joseph Smith for "the temporal salvation of all saints in the last days." (D&C 89:2.)

This revelation, which is called the Word of Wisdom, is

more than just a litany of dietary prohibitions, although many people both within and without the Church tend to view it in that light. In addition to specific restrictions on strong drinks, tobacco, and hot drinks, the Word of Wisdom counsels its adherents to eat grains and herbs, fruits and vegetables, and to eat meat sparingly.

Does that sound like the sort of menu contemporary dietitians would recommend? Absolutely. And they would do so citing scientific research, medical technology, and years of educational background and experience. But Latter-day Saints have been taught to live that healthy lifestyle for generations, and not just because it's better for our bodies. We do it because a prophet of God received a revelation from Heavenly Father in 1833 and promised we would be blessed for our obedience.

And we have been blessed. One study performed by scientists at the University of California at Los Angeles indicates that Latter-day Saints who obey the Word of Wisdom have lower rates of cancer and heart disease when compared to the general United States population.

Dr. James Enstrom of the UCLA School of Public Health explained that the study revealed dramatic differences in the overall mortality rates of health-conscious Mormons who adhere to three particular health practices—that is, never smoking cigarettes, maintaining regular physical activity, and getting regular sleep, which is seven-to-eight hours per day. For instance, a twenty-five-year-old male Church member adhering to these practices would have a life expectancy of eighty-five years, compared to a life expectancy of seventy-four years for a typical United States male. (See "Health Practices and Cancer Mortality Among Active California Mormons," James E. Enstrom, *Journal of the National Cancer Institute*, 6 December 1989, pp. 1807–1814.)

All of this is completely consistent with the profound promise the Lord gave along with the Word of Wisdom back in 1833: "And all saints who remember to keep and do these sayings, walking in obedience to the commandments, shall receive health in their navel and marrow to their bones;

"And shall find wisdom and great treasures of knowledge, even hidden treasures;

"And shall run and not be weary, and shall walk and not faint." (D&C 89:18–20.)

Clearly, the Lord keeps His promises to His children. And just as clearly, the privilege of knowing and receiving the promised blessings of the Word of Wisdom is another of those fruits that come from living the gospel of Jesus Christ.

The Lord's Standard of Sexual Purity

The Church of Jesus Christ of Latter-day Saints teaches the same standard of sexual purity that has been in place among God's people from the beginning of time, including purity of thought, complete sexual abstinence before marriage, and total fidelity within marriage. Following that standard is the only way one can confidently avoid the unfortunate consequences of immorality so prevalent in our society today.

"We declare firmly and unalterably, [morality] is not an outworn garment, faded, old-fashioned, and threadbare," said a modern prophet named Spencer W. Kimball. "God is the same yesterday, today, and forever, and his covenants and doctrines are immutable; and when the sun grows cold and stars no longer shine, the law of chastity will still be basic in God's world and in the Lord's Church. Old values are upheld by the Church not because they are old, but rather because through the ages they have proved right. It will always be the rule." ("President Kimball Speaks Out on Morality," *Ensign*, November 1980, p. 94.)

The Lord's standard of sexual purity isn't just another lifestyle choice in a world rife with worry and paranoia.

Those who choose to live it are spared the emotional consequences of meaningless one-night stands, the spiritual trauma of unrequited commitment, and the inherent moral dilemma of a relationship in which gratification is a higher priority than responsibility. Instead, they open themselves to the remarkable possibilities of a marriage built on a sure foundation of mutual trust, commitment, and respect.

I have officiated at many such marriages, and it is an incredible thing to see and feel the power of purity that radiates from the hearts and souls of young men and women who have been obedient to God's commandments. And what a blessing it is for them to be able to look into the eyes of their loved one knowing that they have saved this most intimate, personal part of themselves for the commitments and covenants of marriage. For those couples sex becomes a form of communication, a way of expressing deep feelings for which there aren't adequate words. It is nature's most sublime way of bonding one human soul to another. And when its desired result is the creation of new life, it allows a man and a woman to join hands with God in fulfilling one of the most important purposes of mortality and one of the key elements of Heavenly Father's eternal plan for His children.

If that sounds old-fashioned, so be it. It also has the benefit of being true. And right. And another delicious bit of fruit from the gospel tree. Just think what the present would be like if all men and women lived this law!

Teaching All Nations

Jesus instructed His disciples to "teach all nations, baptizing them in the name of the Father, and of the Son, and of the Holy Ghost: Teaching them to observe all things whatsoever I have commanded you." (Matthew 28:19–20.) More recently, the Savior taught His latter-day followers that "it becometh every man who hath been warned to warn his neighbor." (D&C 88:81.)

That's why every year thousands of young, single men and women and older couples leave home, family, and friends at their own (or their family's) expense to serve the Lord as missionaries in various parts of the world—even though, to be perfectly candid, most of them feel every bit as uncomfortable standing on your doorstep as you do finding them there. Not only do they have a message of eternal significance to share, but they also have a divine mandate to do so.

That alone should be enough reason for Latter-day Saints to feel strongly about serving as missionaries. But whenever you serve the Lord, He blesses you. Many of our missionaries begin their missions thinking they are going to repay Heavenly Father for His goodness toward them by serving Him for eighteen months or two years. But before long they learn an important eternal truth: You can never do more for the Lord than He can do for you.

Through the years I have watched countless missionaries come and go, and I have seen extraordinary things happen in their lives and in the lives of their families as a result. The work they are called to do is hard and sometimes discouraging. But because they have the assurance that they are on God's errand, they are able to valiantly serve Him. I often suggest to those who want to know if the Church is true that they spend a few hours working with our missionaries. It doesn't take long to learn that no one can do all of the things a missionary does every day without knowing beyond any question that what they are doing is right and true.

The Lord does bless His missionaries just as surely as they bless the lives of those they teach and baptize. Difficult languages are learned with astonishing speed and skill. Financially strapped families back home find unforeseen means to support their missionaries. Weaknesses become strengths, challenges become opportunities, trials become triumphs, and adversity becomes an adventure in the service of the Lord—another fruit of gospel living.

A Lay Ministry

The Church of Jesus Christ of Latter-day Saints doesn't have a paid, professional clergy. Everywhere the Church is organized, it is administered and staffed by members of the ward or branch (which is what we call our congregations) who have been called to their positions through the inspiration of the Holy Spirit. And that's quite an accomplishment, especially when you consider that the Church program for each congregation includes:

—priesthood classes for all men twelve years of age and older;

—the Relief Society, the world's oldest and largest women's organization, which emphasizes and encourages spirituality, service and sisterhood;

—Young Women, an organization for girls twelve through eighteen;

—the Primary, which is responsible for the religious instruction of children under twelve;

—the Sunday School, which is responsible for the scriptural instruction of everyone older than twelve;

—Aaronic priesthood and Scouting programs for boys twelve through eighteen;

—and a vast assortment of other programs and activities, including genealogy (family history research), ward choirs, library resources, social functions, and missionary work.

That's a lot of ground to cover. Maintaining an effective ward organization is a challenging task, and it requires the extraordinary service and efforts of dozens of ward members every year. But it is a real blessing in the lives of those who serve as well as those who are served. The entire program of the Church is designed to give its members a broad range of experiences and opportunities that will help bring them to Christ. A man may serve for five or six years as bishop of the ward, responsible for the spiritual and temporal welfare of five hundred men, women, and children. Then one day he is released, and two weeks later he is teaching seven teenagers in Sunday School.

And that's just as it should be. Assignments in the Church rotate on a regular basis. We serve wherever we're called, and we bless lives in whatever way we can. As we do that, we experience the exhilarating joy of service while drawing closer to our brothers and sisters in the gospel—and, not coincidentally, closer to God.

Of course, service in the Church also creates some special challenges for our members. As you may already be aware, membership in The Church of Jesus Christ of Latter-day Saints isn't a Sunday-only kind of thing, it is a way of life. Consequently, we have things going on during the week that offer opportunities for participation and service: family home evening, youth activities and service projects, temple attendance, ward parties, Cub Scout pack meetings, Relief Society programs, leadership training, and so forth. And because we're so involved in Church and family activities, we're sometimes perceived as being aloof or disinterested in what's going on in our neighborhoods and communities.

Please don't misunderstand: I'm not trying to justify neighborly inaction on our part. We need to be good neighbors and citizens in our communities. If sometimes our members seem to be in a hurry, ask them what it is that keeps them so busy. You will be surprised to learn how much they are doing in so many different areas, including rendering service in the community.

We are active and involved in good things that we hope, in one way or another, will help make the world a better place in which to live. The organization of the Church has a proven track record in responding quickly with emergency supplies and personnel in times of community crisis. And the leadership training and experience provided through our lay ministry has provided communities and service organizations throughout the world with a vast pool of willing, dedicated workers and public servants—yet another fruit of the gospel.

Providing for the Needy in the Lord's Way

Speaking of the final judgment, the Savior taught His followers: "When the Son of man shall come in his glory, and all the holy angels with him, then shall he sit upon the throne of his glory:

"And before him shall be gathered all nations: and he shall separate them one from another, as a shepherd divideth his sheep from the goats:

"And he shall set the sheep on his right hand, but the goats on the left.

"Then shall the King say unto them on his right hand, Come, ye blessed of my Father, inherit the kingdom prepared for you from the foundation of the world:

"For I was an hungred, and ye gave me meat: I was thirsty, and ye gave me drink: I was a stranger, and ye took me in:

"Naked, and ye clothed me: I was sick, and ye visited me: I was in prison, and ye came unto me.

"Then shall the righteous answer him, saying, Lord, when saw we thee an hungred, and fed thee? or thirsty, and gave thee drink?

"When saw we thee a stranger, and took thee in? or naked, and clothed thee?

"Or when saw we thee sick, or in prison, and came unto thee?

"And the King shall answer and say unto them, Verily I say unto you, Inasmuch as ye have done it unto the least of these my brethren, ye have done it unto me." (Matthew 25:31–40.)

In The Church of Jesus Christ of Latter-day Saints, we take that instruction very seriously. A tremendous amount of energy, effort, and resources are expended by the Church on both the local and international levels to provide in the Lord's way for those who are less fortunate. On the first Sunday of every month, Latter-day Saints are urged to fast for two meals, and then to donate the money that would have been expended on those meals to the Church for its various ministries among the world's poor and needy. Many donate much more. That money, called a fast offering, is used for humanitarian purposes.

Those humanitarian purposes, however, are quite diverse. When members of the Church fall on hard economic times, most look first to their families and to the Church for help rather than to public assistance programs. Many services are available through LDS welfare programs to provide assistance, including employment placement, personal counseling, and financial planning. Food and other necessary commodities are available at storage facilities called bishop's storehouses, and in certain situations, the Church can even provide some limited financial assistance. Needy members are given the opportunity to work for the goods and services they receive, thus allowing them to maintain their dignity and make a meaningful contribution to others despite their untoward circumstances.

Helping Others around the World

On a broader scale, the Church is involved in numerous humanitarian projects all around the world. Some of them are ongoing, while others are responsive to immediate needs and concerns, such as flood, earthquake, and famine relief. While Latter-day Saints are widely known for "taking care of our own" through the Church welfare programs, we are also vitally interested in making the world a better, safer, more humane place in which to live.

In 1985, for example, Latter-day Saints observed two special fast days and voluntarily donated approximately six million dollars to be used for humanitarian efforts to relieve suffering and hunger in drought-stricken Africa and elsewhere.

In this instance, I witnessed firsthand the fruits of such giving when the First Presidency of the Church assigned me to travel with the managing director of the Church's Welfare Services to Ethiopia, where we assessed the needs of their people and determined how best to use the collected funds.

Working with several international agencies geared towards dispensing humanitarian aid, we visited remote villages through the arid country. The land was as barren as any I'd ever seen. Topsoil had blown away, and there were no trees or anything green in sight. I'll never forget the lines of women waiting to fill their water jugs, which they would then carefully balance on their shoulders for the long walk home, anywhere from ten to twenty-five miles away.

We visited Red Cross camps and feeding stations where the desperately ill were being cared for. It broke my heart to see so many people suffering. Little children clung to our legs, parents who had sick children brought them to us in the hopes we could do something. Many had open sores or were obviously diseased in some way. Sick mothers were lying on cots trying to feed and comfort their children, many of whom had the sunken eyes and pencil-thin arms and legs of those in the advanced stages of starvation. One older man holding a suffering child begged us to take the boy with us. At a grain distribution station, we saw thousands of human beings waiting their turn to receive a one-hundred-pound sack of wheat. The wheat was placed on the backs of struggling Ethiopians, some of whom were young and able to carry the load. Those who were older, however, staggered under the weight; yet, with their backs bent almost to a ninety-degree angle, they started off on the long trek back to their villages.

I remember stopping in the countryside to eat a small

lunch. When we opened our lunch sacks with sandwiches and fruit, we were soon surrounded by little children who held out their hands, rubbed their stomachs, and touched their lips. There was no way we could eat anything, so we broke our sandwiches into small pieces and distributed them and the fruit among the children.

This visit to Ethiopia was one of the most heart-wrenching of my life, but one that left indelible impressions on my heart and mind. How grateful I was for the principle of the fast and for Church members who had donated so generously and made it possible for us to make sizeable contributions to aid the people of Ethiopia.

The Law of Tithing

As we spoke of the Church's humanitarian efforts and the money Church members donate through their fast offerings, you might have wondered if this is how the Church gets the money it needs to meet its operating expenses. Please allow me to repeat: fast offering donations are used *exclusively* to provide for the poor and the needy. Money for other purposes comes from another kind of member donation called tithing.

The law of tithing has been in place since Old Testament times. We know, for example, that Abraham paid tithing to the great high priest Melchizedek (see Genesis 14:17–20). And the last prophet of the Old Testament, Malachi, warned his people that by not properly paying their tithes and offerings they were, in a sense, robbing God.

"Bring ye all the tithes into the storehouse, that there may be meat in [God's] house." (Malachi 3:10.)

Latter-day Saints are taught to tithe, or to donate, one-tenth of their increase—or income—for the building up of The Church of Jesus Christ of Latter-day Saints. With this money the Church builds and operates chapels, temples, and schools. It provides materials for teaching and training members throughout the world in over one hundred languages. Tithing money is also used to meet the necessary administrative expenses of the international Church and to provide local units with their operating budgets, including paying for utilities and other services.

Tithing funds are considered sacred, and are expended carefully, prayerfully, and judiciously. The Church operates completely debt-free. There is no deficit spending in the Church, and all buildings are paid for before they are dedicated. Those who authorize tithing expenditures never do so without thinking of the sacrifice of those by whom the money is faithfully donated. But we are also mindful of the Lord's assurances to the faithful. According to Malachi, God has promised those who tithe that He will "open you the windows of heaven, and pour you out a blessing, that there shall not be room enough to receive it.

"And I will rebuke the devourer for your sakes, and he shall not destroy the fruits of your ground; neither shall your vine cast her fruit before the time in the field, saith the Lord of hosts.

"And all nations shall call you blessed: for ye shall be a delightsome land, saith the Lord of hosts." (Malachi 3:10–12.)

Once again, the Lord promises wonderful fruit for obedience to gospel teachings.

"By Their Fruits Ye Shall Know Them"

Of course, there are other fruits we could mention. For example:

—the educational fruits of people who believe that "the glory of God is intelligence" (D&C 93:36) and that "whatever principle of intelligence we attain unto in this life, it will rise with us in the resurrection" (D&C 130:18). The Church Education System teaches tens of thousands of high school and college-age youth the gospel through seminary and institute programs that span the globe;

—the fruits of confidence, security, and community that come from belonging to a church that cares about its people enough to assign home teachers and visiting teachers to make regular monthly visits to every home to make sure that everyone who lives there is healthy, happy, and spiritually well;

—the positive fruits that come from living balanced, healthy lives, with as much attention paid to spiritual growth and development as to physical, economic, and social concerns;

—and the collective fruits of lives guided by traditional values of honesty, integrity, morality, sacrifice, and faithfulness.

With these few examples, does it sound like I'm bragging? If so, please forgive me. We don't claim to have a corner on the goodness market. Nor would we pretend to profess that Latter-day Saints live lives free of worldly care and concern. But we honestly and sincerely feel that God has given us something special, something infinitely worth sharing. And that's why I ask you to consider the fruits that come from the lives of members of The Church of Jesus Christ of Latter-day Saints, for as the Savior Himself said: "Ye shall know them by their fruits. Do men gather grapes of thorns, or figs of thistles?

"Even so every good tree bringeth forth good fruit; but a corrupt tree bringeth forth evil fruit.

"A good tree cannot bring forth evil fruit, neither can a corrupt tree bring forth good fruit.

"Every tree that bringeth not forth good fruit is hewn down, and cast into the fire.

"Wherefore by their fruits ye shall know them." (Matthew 7:16–20.)

The Anchor of Faith

Let's return now to the word we considered as we began this journey toward understanding. As a matter of fact, that was the very word: *understanding*.

I indicated in the introduction that my objective in writing this book was "to help those who read these pages—especially those who are not members of The Church of Jesus Christ of Latter-day Saints—better understand the Church and its members."

From that page to this we've covered many theological and historical subjects in our attempt to facilitate understanding. I've discussed our beliefs regarding Jesus Christ and His wondrous life and ministry, and how we believe there was a falling away from His teachings during the first couple of centuries following His death and resurrection. I've also talked about the Restoration of the fulness of the gospel of Jesus Christ through a series of miraculous occurrences, and how gospel truth continues to work miracles in the lives of faithful Latter-day Saints today.

That's a lot to digest—especially in an era when so many people are uncomfortable with the notion of miracles and are suspicious of religious faith in general. While I understand where those suspicions come from (we've all seen news reports of religionists from across the entire theological spectrum who don't practice what they preach), I continue to believe that faith—*real* faith, whole-souled and unshakable—can be as important to a healthy, balanced life as a sturdy anchor is to a ship bound for the open seas. If you've ever seen the anchor on a large ship, you know how massive it is and how sturdy and strong the metal links of the anchor chain are. But when compared to the total size and weight of the entire ship, the anchor and its chain seem small indeed. Still, if properly placed on the bottom of the sea, a sturdy anchor can hold a giant ship fast, even in troubled waters.

That's the same function faith in God serves in the lives of believing Latter-day Saints. Well-founded and carefully maintained, it holds them steady and calm despite the social turbulence and wickedness that swirls around them. Of course, this faith must be more than just lip service, or it won't be strong enough to withstand the stresses placed upon it by contemporary living. In order for our faith to be meaningful and effective as an anchor to our souls, it must be centered on Jesus Christ, His life and His Atonement, and in the restoration of His gospel to the earth through the Prophet Joseph Smith. The eternal principles that I have discussed can also be likened to links of the chain that help us to be anchored to gospel truth.

Is It True?

I'm sure you can see how belief in the things we've talked about would influence every aspect of your life. Knowing and living the gospel of Jesus Christ affects every major decision you make and alters the course of your life because it opens your eyes to new perspectives and insights—especially with regard to your eternal potential— while filling your heart with new feelings and your mind with new understanding. But this takes place only if you really, sincerely believe in Jesus Christ and His gospel.

118

Nevertheless, I understand if all of this seems a bit overwhelming. And while it's true that I can't physically prove to you that these events took place as I have described them, I do testify humbly and sincerely that I have told you the truth. Similarly, you need to know that your Latter-day Saint friends believe with all of their hearts that what I'm telling you is true.

And that's why they do some of the things they do and say some of the things they say. They believe in a religion that is dynamic, based on continuous revelation and eternal progression. Theirs is not a passive belief. It would, after all, be difficult to believe such things and be ambivalent about them. Active Latter-day Saints tend to be very committed to their church and very devoted to their doctrine, not because they think they're any better than anyone else, but because they sincerely believe they have an important message about the restoration of the gospel of Jesus Christ. And they believe it is a message of great gladness and joy that the Lord expects them to share with the entire world.

When I was mission president in Toronto I was invited to participate in a popular radio talk show. No, my missionaries didn't set me up for this one—I accepted this invitation on my own. After some initial discussion of the similarities between The Church of Jesus Christ of Latter-day Saints and other Christian denominations, the host asked this significant question: "What makes your church different from other churches?"

"Let me answer your question with another question," I replied. "If Moses were on the earth today, would you be interested in what he had to say?"

"Of course," the talk show host responded. "*Everyone* would be interested."

"Well, that's our message to the world," I said. "There is a prophet of God on the earth today who has the same power and authority that Moses had. God directs His Church through His prophet today, just as He did in Moses' day."

My host was silent for a moment—which, as you know, can seem like forever on the radio.

"You're right," he said at last. "That *is* different."

So yes, we're different. But it is an important difference—especially because it is true. And that's one thing you can definitely say about everything we have talked about: either it is true or it is not. Either Joseph Smith had that remarkable vision we call the First Vision, or he did not. Either he translated the Book of Mormon by the gift and power of God, or he did not. Either the priesthood of God was restored to earth through the ministry of John the Baptist, Peter, James, and John, or it was not. Either Heavenly Father created a wonderful eternal plan for His children, or He did not. Either the principles embodied in the Articles of Faith represent revealed truth, or they do not. Either the fruits of Mormonism are the natural consequences of obedience to God's commandments, or they are not.

There really aren't a lot of options, are there? Either these things happened as I've indicated, or they did not. If they didn't happen, then a lot of us have really been fooled. But if they did happen, I'm sure you can see how important it would be for that information to be shared with all men and women, everywhere. In fact, can you think of anything more important to know than this?

You May Ask of God

It's important to me that you know that I know that what I'm telling you is true. My witness is that Joseph Smith did, in fact, look up through that grove of trees, and God the Father and His Son Jesus Christ did appear and speak to him, as Joseph's testimony records. The Angel Moroni subsequently placed in the young Joseph's possession plates of gold, which not only gave an account of an ancient people who lived on the American Continent but provided another testament of Jesus Christ.

I testify that John the Baptist, the same Baptist who baptized his cousin, Jesus, in the River Jordan, appeared as a resurrected man on the banks of the Susquehanna River, laid his hands upon the head of Joseph Smith, and conferred upon him the Aaronic Priesthood. I know that Peter, James, and John—those same Apostles who were called by Jesus of Nazareth—appeared a short time later and conferred upon Joseph Smith the holy Melchizedek Priesthood. And from that point forward, the fulness of the Restoration of the gospel of Jesus Christ came forth, which I witness to the world is found in The Church of Jesus Christ of Latter-day Saints. The gospel of Jesus Christ has been restored, fully and completely. These things I know!

Because of these simple truths my life and the lives of others who believe as I do are unalterably changed—today and forever. Because we believe that Joseph Smith was a prophet of God and that there is a living prophet on the earth today along with living Apostles of the Lord Jesus Christ (of which I am one), we know and feel the peace and confidence that comes from understanding and living Heavenly Father's eternal plan. We're part of it, each one of us. That makes you and all of us special, no matter what we may now believe. But when we understand the full nature of our relationship with God and His Son Jesus Christ, certain possibilities become more focused and certain responsibilities become more clear. That's why we care, and why we feel such a need to share the gospel with every son and daughter of God.

The challenge for you and me is exactly as it was for the minister who asked me the question I referred to earlier: "Mr. Ballard, if you would just place the Gold Plates on the table, then we would know whether or not what you are telling us is true."

My reply is still the same, that God does not reveal His word that way. But, thankfully, there *is* a way that all of God's children can know—and I mean really *know*—for themselves that what I've said is true. I'm not just talking about believing me or taking my word for it or anything like that. What I'm talking about is going right to the source of all truth to find out once and for all if what I've told you is true.

In the last chapter of the Book of Mormon, Moroni made a significant promise to those who would one day read the things that are written in that sacred book of scripture. I believe the same promise applies to sincere seekers of truth in any forum or pursuit:

"And when ye shall receive these things, I would exhort you that ye would ask God, the Eternal Father, in the name of Christ, if these things are not true; and if ye shall ask with a sincere heart, with real intent, having faith in Christ, he will manifest the truth of it unto you, by the power of the Holy Ghost.

"And by the power of the Holy Ghost ye may know the truth of all things." (Moroni 10:4–5.)

Moroni's promise is strikingly similar to the passage in James that motivated the fourteen-year-old Joseph Smith to seek answers from God to remedy his religious confusion: "If any of you lack wisdom, let him ask of God, that giveth to all men liberally, and upbraideth not; and it shall be given him." (James 1:5.)

Both James and Moroni urge us to go directly to the Source of Truth for answers to our questions. If we seek Him humbly and sincerely, He will help us discern truth from error. As the Savior Himself assured His disciples: "And ye shall know the truth, and the truth shall make you free " (John 8:32.)

But how will we know?

Experiment upon the Words of Christ

Once again, the Book of Mormon provides some wonderful insights. The prophet Alma wisely counseled those seeking the truth—including those who "can no more than desire to believe"—to conduct "an experiment upon my words":

"Now, we will compare the word unto a seed. Now, if ye give place, that a seed may be planted in your heart, behold, if it be a true seed, or a good seed, if ye do not cast it out by your unbelief, that ye will resist the Spirit of the Lord, behold, it will begin to swell within your breasts; and when you feel these swelling motions, ye will begin to say within yourselves—It must needs be that this is a good seed, or that the word is good, for it beginneth to enlarge my soul; yea, it beginneth to enlighten my understanding, yea, it beginneth to be delicious to me." (Alma 32:27–28.)

And that is all anyone can ask you to do: to "experiment" upon the words of Christ, to "give place, that a seed may be planted in your heart" and to not "resist the Spirit of the Lord." It is my sincere belief that if you will do those things and ask Heavenly Father in prayer if they are true, He will tell you. That is His promise to you and to all of His children.

"Behold," Jesus said through John, "I stand at the door, and knock: if any man will hear my voice, and open the door, I will come in to him, and will sup with him, and he with me.

"To him that overcometh will I grant to sit with me in my throne, even as I also overcame, and am set down with my Father in his throne." (Revelation 3:20–21.)

Please don't let this opportunity to receive personal revelation from God pass. Consider what I've written here. Weigh it carefully. Measure it against the things you believe—and the things you *want* to believe. Hold fast to all that you know to be true and add to that the fulness of the restored gospel of Jesus Christ. Take into account what you've felt as you've read these words. Then put it all to the ultimate test: Ask God. Listen for His answer with your heart, then respond to what you feel.

If you will do so, my simple faith tells me you'll receive the answers you're looking for. And you'll understand—more intimately, perhaps, than you thought you might—why your LDS friends are so motivated to share what they know to be true. With millions of members living in all parts of the planet and tens of thousands of missionaries serving throughout the world, you are never far away from answers to any questions that you may now have. Please feel free to contact me personally (at 47 E. South Temple, Salt Lake City, Utah 84150) if I can be of help, and I will do all that I can to help you learn and understand more fully our message to the world.

After all, "understanding" is what we were trying to accomplish back when we first started.

God bless you, my friend!

Index